Country Wreaths
from Caprilands

To all the Caprilands creative crew.

Country Wreaths from Caprilands

The Legend, Lore and Design of Traditional Herbal Wreaths

Adelma Grenier Simmons

Photographed by
Randa Bishop

RODALE PRESS
Emmaus, Pennsylvania

For information, address: Rodale Press
33 East Minor Street, Emmaus, PA 18098

Photographs by Randa Bishop
Photographs copyright © 1988 by Randa Bishop

Published by Rodale Press
33 East Minor Street, Emmaus, PA 18098

Editorial development and design by Combined Books
26 Summit Grove Avenue, Suite 207, Bryn Mawr, PA 19010

Produced by Wieser & Wieser
118 East 25th Street, New York, NY 10010

Library of Congress Cataloging-in-Publication Data

Simmons, Adelma Grenier.
  Country wreaths from Caprilands: the legend, lore, and design of traditional herbal wreaths / Adelma Grenier Simmons; photos by Randa Bishop.
  ISBN 0-87857-792-0 (hardcover)
  1. Wreaths. 2. Wreaths—Folklore. 3. Herbs—Utilization.
4. Aromatic plants—Utilization. 5. Caprilands Herb Farm (Coventry, Conn.) I. Title. II. Title: Herbal wreaths.
SB449.5.W74S55 1988
745.92—dc19   88-11343
                                                                    CIP

  2   4   6   8   10   9   7   5   3   1   hardcover

Contents

Of Airy elves by moonlight shadows seen
The silver token and the circled green
Of virgins visited by angel powers
With golden crowns and wreaths of heavenly flowers
—*Alexander Pope*

Preface

It was the romantic aspect of herbs that first lured me—their histories, their meanings, and the beauty they add to the landscape. Out of this interest came the desire to create a country retreat for people who yearn to delve into history, to experience the uses of herbs, or simply to wander through herb gardens. Since 1929 when we first found our old farm and named it Caprilands, we have sought to show people how they can enrich their lives through the joys of herbs.

Wreath making is one of the ways we can enjoy herbs and their meanings. Wreaths hold significance not only because of the herbs used to make them but also because of their connection to holidays and historical events. Behind the stirring of the seasons, events shape around special days that mark the birth, death, or life of holy and influential people. These periods of celebration give a greater meaning to life. My early interest in wreaths came from the desire to celebrate these memorable days with special decorations.

In this book, I want to share with you the pleasures of wreaths and the herbal lore surrounding them. I want to give you some new ideas for making country wreaths using the wealth of materials that can be grown in your garden or gathered from the countryside. You will discover not only wreaths but chaplets—wreaths worn on the head. You will learn about garlands—strings of flowers or leaves that are hung around doorways or coiled around banisters for decoration.

I have also included practical information on growing, gathering, and preserving wreath materials, as well as techniques for making the wreaths sturdy. Now you can make your own attractive, fragrant, long-lasting creations.

7

I

WREATHS THROUGH THE AGES

Wreaths had far more significance in the past than most of us realize. Today we decorate with them, often limiting their use to holiday times. But in other ages, wreaths carried meaning and served many uses. They signified honor and success and were awarded to important people as recognition of their achievements. Certain wreaths were hung to protect the home from evil and harm. Others were thought to have therapeutic properties and were worn by the sick.

Not only did wreaths carry significance, but the specific herbs, greens, and flowers used in these wreaths had meaning. For example, rosemary signified remembrance; bay leaves symbolized success; roses, of course, meant love. By looking back into the history of wreaths and to the meanings of herbs and flowers, the wreaths we create today will have more meaning, and making them will be more enjoyable.

When Gods and Goddesses Ruled the Earth

Long before the first century, in Greece, as dawn broke in the cities, young women walked into the busy marketplaces, bringing their country wreaths, garlands, and chaplets to sell. They sold them at the baths where, according to Athenaeus, an early Greek scholar, "shoppers, all bathed, babble before it is bright daylight in the wreath market, while others gabble at the perfume booths over mint and larkspur." Many of the young men, suffering from a night of revelry, sought renewal in the baths and bought wreaths or chaplets to soothe their heads. The scholar could buy a wreath for wisdom or one made of clean, pure, penetrating mint and sweet, memory-giving rosemary to clear his brain. The lover might purchase a floral garland of roses and lilies or a wreath of myrtle, which meant love.

In the civilizations of ancient Greece and Rome, wreaths had all sorts of uses and meanings. At festivals, people wore wreaths on their heads and garlands around their necks. The fragrances of the flowers and herbs perfumed the air around the guests while they lounged on couches, entertained by musicians, acrobats, and singers. Flowers were plucked from chaplets and dropped into goblets of wine when toasting or pledging the health of guests and friends.

A rosemary wreath improved the memory.   *A wreath of myrtle signified love.*

In ancient Rome and Greece partygoers wore wreaths.

Beyond fun and festivity, wreaths held significance as symbols of victory and accomplishment. Wreaths were crowns of glory. In contests, they were awarded as prizes to the winners. Olive wreaths donned the heads of the victors at the Greek games of Panathenaia and Olympia, pine wreaths were awarded at Isthmia, laurel at Delphi, and celery at Nemia. For the more serious victories of wars and battles, oak leaves—a symbol of greatness and battles won—crowned warriors and civic leaders. According to Pliny, a Roman naturalist and scholar (A.D. 23–79), no crown was more glorious than a crown of common grasses. During battles, when an army had just escaped disaster, soldiers would award their general a crown made from grass gathered at the spot where the troops had been rescued from defeat. Only by the acclamation of the whole army was such a crown given.

*An oak wreath once symbol-
ized greatness and battles won.*

Scholars, for their accomplishments, also wore wreaths. Traditionally poets and artists donned ivy, and statesmen wore their laurels.
Later this tradition changed; poets wore laurel and in their verse
crowned revelers with ivy. The laurel used for crowns was not always
Laurus nobilis, also commonly known as sweet bay. At times Alex-
andrian laurel *(Ruscus racemosus)* was chosen for its broader leaves. Its
foliage conveniently concealed the balding head of Julius Caesar.

Pliny described perhaps one of the most glorious crowns: "The
Helichrysus [our strawflower] has a flower resembling gold in appearance, a small leaf and a slender, fine, but hard, stem. According to
the Magi the person who crowns himself with a chaplet of this flower
and takes his unguents from a box of gold, of the kind generally
known as apyron, will be sure to secure esteem and glory among his
fellow men, such are the flowers of spring."

While certain wreaths symbolized power and glory, others had
power, or so the ancient Greeks and Romans thought. They hung them

In ancient Rome, poets, artists, and statesmen wore laurels to signify their accomplishments. At Caprilands, we hang festive laurels on plows to celebrate the importance of this implement.

Strawflowers once made glorious crowns. In modern times we use strawflowers (the three large deep-toned flowers) to adorn decorative brooms and other flower crafts.

in their homes on doors and windows and on the altars of their shrines to lure kind spirits and to keep out evil ones.

The power of plants was greatly respected, and plants for crowns and garlands were chosen carefully. People believed that certain plants emitted odors that could damage the brain. Pliny warned that stocks excited the brain, and marjoram stupefied it. Other plants, such as roses, anemones, violets, carnations, and lilies supposedly had therapeutic properties. Mint and rosemary wreaths were used to clear the mind and improve memory. To prevent intoxication at banquets, Romans wore wreaths made from linden tree bark woven with flowers, and myrtle supposedly had the power to dispel the fumes and effects of wine.

Wreaths and the materials of wreaths had great significance. With time some of these uses and meanings changed, but the popularity and importance of wreaths and garlands and herbs and flowers continued through the ages.

When Knights Were Bold and Maidens Fair

Wreaths were also an important part of the culture of the Middle Ages. Their uses can be seen in Medieval songs and paintings. Many of these uses reflect those of ancient Rome and Greece. In the ancient world, wreaths crowned the heads of deities; the artwork of the Middle Ages shows wreaths adorning the Virgin Mary and the saints. Jousting contenders are pictured with crowns like those awarded for valor in Roman games. In romantic paintings, couples recline in castle gardens, wearing crowns of leaves, and the damsel is often depicted making or presenting a wreath of flowers to her lover.

Roses and wheat were associated with the legend of St. Barbara and are used at Caprilands in the St. Barbara's wreath.

The wreath makers of that time gathered plants from the herb garden or from surrounding meadows. In monasteries the monks, who cultivated herbs and flowers as well as fruits and vegetables, came to associate growing plants with the traditions of the church. In time, many plants became associated with specific saints, either because they were prevalent at the season of the year when the saint's day occurred or because they were connected with a legend of the saint's life. These plants then were used in garlands and wreaths for religious festivals and celebrations that honored the saints. By looking at these celebrations as well as others that occur throughout the seasons, we can appreciate the historical uses and meanings of wreaths.

St. George's Day

One of the principal celebrations of spring in central and eastern Europe was St. George's Day. Every year on the eve of April 23, the country people of Transylvania and Romania would cut down a young willow tree, sink it into the ground, and decorate it with wreaths and garlands. The young and the old gathered around the tree to witness the dance of Green George, the central figure of the festival. Covered from head to toe in green leaves, his antics ensured the rain needed for plentiful crops in the season ahead.

Green George, covered from head to toe with willow branches, danced to celebrate spring and to ensure bountiful crops.

In Alsace, France, people celebrated St. George's Day with a procession. A gathering of villagers walked through the streets from house to house, singing songs of spring and collecting gifts for the church. Among the group, a little girl dressed in white carried a small tree or branch covered with flowers, garlands, and ribbons. People believed that God was present in the bough and that the procession brought God's blessing for a good growing year to each house. Some of the songs and chants suggested that the householders should give freely or their crops would not grow—their seeds would be eaten by birds, and their vines would bear no fruit. Those who refused to contribute would not receive the blessings that the decorated green bough bestowed.

May Day

When May 1 arrives, people all over the world celebrate May Day; however, this was not always true. In Northern Europe, May Day festivities blended into St. George's Day, April 23. During the Middle Ages and through the Renaissance, May Day fell on May 12, according to our present calendar. By this time, spring had arrived in the British Isles. It was warm enough to spend the night in the woods and return in the morning laden with flowers, boughs, and branches for making garlands and crowns.

During the Reformation, May Day observances were banned, but with the Restoration the celebrations returned and continued in many towns until the beginning of the 20th century. About this time the festivals lost much of their relationship to planting and became largely children's festivals; however, the traditions of crowning the May queen

The top of the maypole is traditionally adorned with a wreath. The doll is a special addition to this English maypole.

After the Reformation, May Day was more a children's festival than one celebrating spring planting.

and king and making May baskets and garlands did survive. The custom of crowning the May queen has lasted at least since the 1500s when Spenser wrote the following poem:

> *See where she sits upon the grassie greene,*
> *A seemly sight*
> *Ye clad in scarlet like a maiden Queen,*
> *And ermines white,*
> *And on her head a crimson coronet.*
> *With Daffodils and Damask Roses set;*
> *Bay leaves betweene*
> *And Primroses greene*
> *Embellished the sweete Violet.*
>
> *—Edmund Spenser*

During the traditional May Day celebration, young men raced to the Maypole, and the first to reach it was crowned King of the May. The men scrambled to the top of the pole, where the garlands and the May wreath hung. They crowned the king with the wreath, and all obeyed his orders for the day. The last runner to arrive at the pole became the clown. He then performed all sorts of antics to amuse the crowd.

Villagers built the Maypole from a tall, straight pine or hawthorne. In many towns and villages it stood in place and was simply redecorated every year. Its name did not come from the month of May but from the word *mai,* meaning floral or green. In time, the hawthorne tree itself became known as the *mai.* Hawthornes bloom during the season of the May Day festival, and their beautiful white blossoms and those of the lily of the valley were used extensively in garlands and chaplets for May Day festivities.

A fresh wreath of daisies is an appropriate May Day decoration.

Whitsunday

Also known as Pentecost, Whitsunday arrived 50 days after Easter and was the day when church confirmations took place. Young people in procession carried garlands through the village to the church and placed them at the altar. They made these garlands for "White Sunday" from sweet flags, lilies of the valley, roses, and other white flowers, with sweet woodruff for fragrance.

Midsummer Day

Midsummer Day, June 24, honors St. John the Baptist and falls close to the ancient celebration of the summer solstice on June 21. St. John was reputedly born at midnight on June 24, and so his name and legend have become part of the Midsummer celebration. Traditionally, people have considered midsummer a magical time. According to one legend, at precisely midnight the fern, which has no flowers or seeds, blooms and produces invisible magic seeds. Anyone who gathers them at that moment can be rendered invisible. Supposedly fairies and demons engaged in fierce combat for possession of these magic seeds.

In keeping with this magical mood, the flowers used in midsummer garlands had to be picked before the dew had dried and the sun had driven away its magic. White lilies, green birch, fennel, St.-John's-wort, and wormwood made up garlands that were hung over doors and windows. Other garlands woven from vervain and flax were suspended from ceilings inside the houses.

In 16th century Germany, in the villages, people built bonfires on the eve of St. John. Young and old gathered around, danced, sang, and prayed, wearing chaplets made from mugwort and vervain, which they believed protected them against misfortune.

White flowers, such as roses, are traditional Whitsunday decorations.

Ferns, daisies, and mugwort make a Midsummer wreath.

Harvest Time

With fall comes harvest, and for farm people this time has always brought out the festive spirit. Harvest rituals and practices of early times varied from country to country yet shared themes of gratefulness for good harvests and hope for future prosperity. In many countries, farmers fashioned dolls from the last sheaf of grain that was harvested. Dressed to resemble a woman, this doll symbolized the fruitfulness of the earth and was awarded to the farmer who first finished harvesting his fields.

From the fruit of the last sheaf, whether it be ears of corn or stalks of wheat, a wreath was made and decorated with field flowers. The prettiest young girl in the area wore this wreath and led the farmers and villagers in procession to the house of the squire, where everyone enjoyed the good food and dancing of the harvest festival. Afterward the wreath was hung on the wall until the next spring, when the farmers would pluck the kernels of grain and mix them with the seed for the spring planting.

Today harvest dolls are decorative elements displayed in the fall. They may be simply made of raffia and straw or more elaborately made by wheat weaving.

Harvest rituals varied from country to country. In Gloucestershire, England, it was a time of festive celebration.

Now That Men Are Fair and Women Bold

Today, at Caprilands, we celebrate the changing seasons and the holidays and special events that occur in each season. We celebrate many of the saint's days. St. John's Day, or Midsummer Day, is a special time at Caprilands. The herb gardens are in their prime, and visitors come and go in a steady stream. People find here a place for the quiet enjoyment of growing things as well as the festivity of our summer celebration.

For our celebrations we create wreaths and garlands for decoration. We look to the wreaths and garlands of the past, to the decorations of the festivals of saint's days, and often follow their motifs in creating our own. History becomes intertwined with our wreaths as the wreath maker weaves together herbs and flowers with old, and sometimes ancient. meanings.

We have come full circle in this art. For most of the 20th century, the word "wreath" conjured up visions of rings of evergreen with red ribbons hung on doors at Christmas time. But now we have returned to the origins of this craft. We make these decorations with artemisia, yarrow, baby's breath, rose buds, bay leaves, and many other herbs and flowers.

The history and symbolism of these herbs and flowers and of the wreaths themselves add a new dimension to the craft of wreath making and to our enjoyment of the finished work. As we prepare and shape herbs and flowers into wreaths, their stories and meanings enrich the hours and inspire our hands.

A summer harvest wreath may be made from corn leaves and tassels.

II

THE WREATHS
AND GARLANDS
OF CAPRILANDS

People did not always show enthusiasm for the wreaths we make at Caprilands. In the 1930s, when we began making them, dried herbal wreaths were an oddity. Housekeepers decorated their homes with pinecone wreaths because they were neat. Nothing dropped from them; no tiny white ghostly blossoms drifted around the room; and no bits of material littered the floor. When we showed people our wreaths they often exclaimed, "Why, it's all dry!" Our greatest shock, however, came from a friend we thought would be delighted with one of our wreaths because it was a gift of herbs and flowers that would last indefinitely in her city apartment. We carefully chose materials, and two of us labored over the wreath until we considered it perfect. Then we carefully padded and wrapped it and mailed it to her apartment in New York City. We awaited an enthusiastic reply. After a long period, the letter came. It was brief and cut us to the quick. It said, "I regret to state that the wreath you sent was completely dry upon arrival and we had to dispose of it." Other times, other ways!

That was our most discouraging experience. Fortunately we were convinced that our efforts would eventually be appreciated, as indeed they have been. Today it is difficult to supply the demand. We work throughout the year, creating beauty from a variety of herbs, many of which were once despised as weeds.

Caprilands wreaths are truly creations from the herb garden. We use herbal material from the base to the finished design. Even the evergreens we use are herbal—juniper, pine, red cedar, eucalyptus, broom, or boxwood. Our silver, brown, or yellow bases are made of several varieties of artemisias. We create the colorful patterns of our wreaths with flowers, fruit, and seedpods of such plants as tansy, goldenrod, roses, American holly, salvias, lavender, amaranth, statice, teasel, and bittersweet. All of these materials had special herbal uses and meanings in the past, which still hold true today.

Wreath making involves a good deal of time, effort, and creativity, so we try to construct wreaths that will last. We build sturdy bases and decorate them with plants, flowers, and spices that will weather well. Some of our kitchen wreaths can be rinsed of dust, dried, and used again.

We once had a very handsome pair of large silver king artemisia wreaths decorated with tansy, yarrow, a few strawflowers, and pearly everlastings. Year after year, we brought them to flower shows to display. Everyone knew that they were not for sale; they were good luck symbols. Each year we refreshed them with some new material placed over the old, and with the passing years, the wreaths became bigger and bigger. They went to ten flower shows as a pair until one of our helpers listened to the plea of a customer and sold one of them.

You'll find wreaths like these as well as some of our other most popular designs described on the following pages. For specific information on wreath materials and construction, see Part III.

Pinecones and nuts combine to make a sturdy wreath with bold form and texture.

Herb gardens contain plants that are both decorative and fragrant as well as edible. Preserving these plants in wreaths means you can enjoy them for many years.

Kitchen Herb Wreaths

We make our kitchen wreaths only from culinary herbs that can be removed and used to season foods. Thyme makes up the bulk of the wreath. It is easy to grow, and therefore abundant, and its sweetness lasts long after it has dried. To the thyme we add rosemary, sage, savory, dill, and parsley. For floral interest we decorate with the edible blossoms of pot marigold (*Calendula officinalis*).

The herbs may be bunched and tied directly to a wire base, although we prefer to attach them to an artemisia base or an edible base. For the latter, we bind stalks of dill together with wire. A six- or eight-inch base is large enough. If these are prepared in the last days of the garden, they will dry in good color for Christmas gifts. Hung in the kitchen, sprigs can be used for seasoning all winter long. For a more elaborate kitchen wreath, we may add some sticks of cinnamon tied in a bow and attached at the base. We might attach little bags of spices, incorporating them into the design, so that they can be removed easily without destroying the pattern.

Bind stalks of dill to create an edible wreath base.

Another kitchen wreath, the tarragon wreath, is very fragrant and can also be used in cooking. On a thin artemisia base or a base made of twisted tarragon stems, we push in small bunches of green tarragon. Then we wire bay leaves onto the wreath in a pattern. Next we puncture cardamom seeds with wire, collect them in bunches like berries, and wire these into the base. We tuck in sprigs of rosemary, and finish the wreath with a plaid bow.

It's not necessary to attach fresh herbs to an artemisia or edible base. Bunch the fresh herbs together, and tie them to a wire base.

Herb Wreaths

One of our herb wreaths is simply made of camomile, caraway, and dill inserted in a base of braided grasses. The grasses are braided on a circle of wire for shape and stability. We pick the camomile when it is thick and green and tie it into little bunches. We often use white ribbons and tie them just beneath the white camomile flowers for greater emphasis. The ends of the bunches are inserted into the braid of grasses. After the camomile bunches have been placed, we insert the brown and green heads of caraway and dill into the braid to make a thick covering. A few daisies or black-eyed Susans add a bright accent.

The most practical herb wreath is one that is completely edible. Pull off the herbs as needed to season foods.

Herb and Spice Wreath

The best known and the most representative of all the Caprilands wreaths is the herb and spice wreath. A fragrant circle of silver king artemisia, bay leaves, and spices, it is both decorative and useful. Every part of the wreath, except for the artemisia base, can be used to season foods.

I made the first herb and spice wreath as a Christmas gift for a friend. In my friend's house, rare old prints and textiles covered the walls; little space remained for a decorative gift. I feared the wreath would be discarded. My friend, however, was a fine cook and used

Cardamom adds white highlights to the herb and spice wreath, the best known of all of the wreaths from Caprilands.

*Small, attractive kitchen
wreaths can be made from a
single culinary herb such as
the sage used here.*

herbs and spices in many recipes long before herb cookery was popular.
As I considered all of this, my design became a working pattern for a
usable gift, not a troublesome decoration.

   After making the base from artemisia, I attached a ring of bay
leaves, wired together in flat bunches of three or four so that they could
be removed to season sauces and soups. Bay leaves signify honor—most
appropriate for my distinguished friend. In the center of each bunch of
bays, I fastened three whole nutmegs, drilled and wired together.
These, of course, could be used for Christmas eggnog, custard pie,
baked apples, and many other dishes. Next came cinnamon sticks,
which I also cut, drilled, and wired in bunches of three. Cardamom, a
wonderful seasonal spice, added a bright touch to the dark color of the
nutmegs and cinnamon sticks, but attaching the cardamom seeds
securely was a problem. I soon found I could pierce them with wire
(the heaviest florist's wire will do this adequately) and gather them
together in small bunches. Rosemary, the herb of remembrance, added
a touch of green to this dried wreath. It has an unmistakable holiday
fragrance, both sweet and gingery. At this point we still hadn't added
all the typical herbs and spices used in Christmas cooking, so we

placed anise, caraway, and coriander in small cellophane bags and tied them to the wreath under a green and brown velvet bow.

Some years after making our first herb and spice wreath, we found that we had created a very desirable item. The demand for these wreaths grew rapidly. We would work far into the night in our farmhouse kitchen, warmed by the old cast-iron range and kept awake by changing the 78 records on the Victrola, while the dogs slept on the scattered remnants of artemisia. The next day all the wreaths we had piled up sold very quickly.

I soon realized that we needed help to fill our orders. We recruited one, then another, and eventually a third assistant. We sped up our wreath assembly by organizing materials, sorting the bay leaves carefully to find those that weren't broken, and drilling and wiring the cinnamon sticks, nutmegs, and cardamom seeds. Even with all this preparation, it took over two hours to finish a wreath.

Today, new workers at Caprilands make these wreaths. They are a bit more decorative and somewhat less functional. At Christmas time we add evergreens, especially juniper, and red berries. But we still make the original herb and spice wreath, designed to be used in cooking. These are the most difficult of our wreaths to assemble, but you can easily freshen them with new rosemary, artemisia, and a bow or bunches of cinnamon sticks and nutmegs. Interestingly, for all the care we take in making this wreath useful, few people ever take it apart because it is such a lovely kitchen decoration.

This kitchen wreath is made from sprigs of thyme.

Incense Wreath

As the name implies, the Caprilands incense wreath is the most fragrant of all our wreaths and contains the most unusual materials. The whole wreath glows with warm autumn colors and is quite redolent. For the base we start with silver king artemisia. The tipping (the covering of the base that becomes the foundation of the pattern) is done with fragrant grasses interspersed with artemisia curls. Then we lace the base with some sweet Annie (*Artemisia annua*) and a little sweet grass. Lavender foliage, dried sweet woodruff, and bunches of dried tarragon are interwoven with the sweet grasses. Next we group

Frankincense and myrrh add aroma to a wreath made of a host of fragrant materials.

Two important ingredients of the incense wreath are tonka beans and cinnamon sticks, bunched together and wired to the base.

together bunches of tonka beans, which smell like new-mown hay, and cinnamon sticks and wire them into the base. Small pieces of sweet-smelling sandalwood surround the circle, and we decorate the wreath with vetiver, which looks like a bleached autumn grass and is one of the most fragrant of the materials used. To complete the design, we attach a bow and tie in two small bags of frankincense and myrrh. These can easily be removed and burned as incense.

Victorian Wreaths

The inspiration for Caprilands Victorian wreaths came from recollections of my childhood visits to our grandparents' "Big House," as we called it, in Vermont. I sometimes opened the sliding door of their Victorian parlor and crept into this dimly lit room, with its formal haircloth furniture, "whatnots" in the corners, and the mantle draped with ball-fringe velvet. Above the mantle and on the tables were wreaths made in memory of departed family members. Very often they were constructed of dried funeral flowers. Afraid of being discovered, I looked at them quickly. Outside, the wind seemed to sigh in the tall spruce trees, a pleasing requiem for the solemnity of the setting. Because of these sad associations, I designed the Victorian wreath to be especially bright, fragrant, and dainty, belying its gloomy origin.

To complete a Victorian wreath, tie a potpourri of lavender, sweet violets, and lilacs into the bow.

For these wreaths we use a fine base of the whitest and best silver king artemisia with tips that look like a border of silver lace. We choose the best curls for the tipping. Our original designs were lavishly decorated with pearly everlasting, the daintiest strawflowers, and bits of green fern. To finish them we attached tiny velvet bows of pink, mauve, and lime green.

Today one of the most sought after of all the Victorians is a wreath solid with flowers. This is really a molded design and requires an extravagant amount of dried flowers.

To make a Victorian wreath, we use a large quanity of strawflowers, pearly or sweet everlastings, small yarrows, pink globe amaranth, blue salvia, and dried rosebuds wired together to make small sweet-smelling bunches. Lavender flowers may be used for fragrance, but keep in mind that when dried, they have very little color. If it's color you want, use blue salvia. Bits of privet or boxwood add a touch of green, but we prefer rosemary; it has a lovely fragrance and looks good even after it has dried.

Many of the flowers for this wreath need special wiring before they are inserted into the design. Strawflowers can be purchased with wires already inserted. If you grow them in your garden, you will have to do this task ahead of time.

The color scheme of a Victorian wreath can vary, but the most appropriate one includes soft pinks, very pale yellows, white, light blue, lime green, and all shades of mauve—the prevalent color of this time period known as the "mauve decade." You can tie bits of faded antique lace into the bow, or conceal a small potpourri of lavender, sweet violets, and lilacs in the knot for fragrance.

Weave ribbons through the flowers and foliage of a Victorian or bridal whimsy.

Wedding Crowns

I have a crown
Of silvered leaves
And when my love and I are wed
His mother shall have my silver crown.
                              —*Latvian song*

Historically, brides wore wreaths as wedding crowns. In Latvian tradition, the crown became a valued heirloom and was handed down from one generation to another. These crowns might be simple—a slender chaplet braided from wild leaves and flowers—or elaborate—a circlet of silver Russian olive leaves. All held importance, and all signified virginity. At Caprilands we make a variety of floral adornments for brides.

Bridal wreaths combine silk roses with dried herbs and flowers.

At Caprilands, we make a variety of floral adornments for brides.

Midsummer Wreath

> On Midsummer Night, I wove
> A wreath of garden flowers,
> Of roses and daisies,
> Of waxen marigolds.
> —Latvian song

Midsummer Day, June 24, is a very special day to many northern Europeans. This is the time when the sun is highest in the heavens and all nature is at its best. Europeans celebrate it with songs and special music. Pagan and Christian beliefs commingle in rituals performed for good luck, good crops, fertile fields, and healthy families.

In the past, many interesting traditions surrounded the celebration of Midsummer Day. One celebration had at its center a fire festival. Participants in this festival wore wreaths made of mugwort (*Artemisia vulgaris*). When singed by fire, the mugwort reputedly became magical. Certain words uttered over it could drive away all evil, and good luck would abound for the coming year.

Another ancient Midsummer tradition was to crown the dairy animals with special wreaths and garlands, as told in this Latvian poem:

> Come quickly, Midsummer Night,
> Many await your arrival.
> The cow awaits a crown of greens
> The girls, a night of revelry.

Villagers made these crowns from wildflowers, clover, and grasses, and the garlanded animals walked in the midsummer festival parades.

Mugwort was an important herb in Midsummer celebrations.

This cow no longer "awaits a crown of greens." Made of wildflowers, clover, and grasses, this wreath is beautiful and an edible treat for Bossy.

Today, at Caprilands we all wear wreaths at our Midsummer celebration and strew rushes, rose petals, lavender, and fragrant herbs on the floors. We make our crowns from both mugwort and cinnamon ferns, the two principal plants of midsummer. Although it is easy to form a wreath from mugwort alone, combining it with cinnamon ferns is more difficult. Because we make wreaths for all of our thousand guests, we form the basic crown from ferns and insert a small piece of mugwort in each one. The ferns are attractive, easy to work with, and they smell fresh and sweet. According to legend, our wreaths will ensure good luck for another year.

Lammas Day Wreath

When weary reapers quit the sultry field,
And crowned with corn,
Their thanks to Ceres yield the above.
                                        —*Alexander Pope*

Lammas Day, August 1, originated with the worship of Ceres (or Demeter), the goddess of planting and harvesting. On this day, the first grains harvested were baked into bread as an offering to the goddess.

At Caprilands on Lammas Day, we craft a wreath of wheat and crown our statue of Ceres.

In Christian churches the first wheat was blessed and baked into a communion loaf to be used at the "Loaf Mass." Lammas Day was a time to dedicate the first fruits of the harvest to the church. After placing the crops in the chancel for a special blessing, the community offered prayers of thanks for the abundance of the harvest.

At Caprilands on Lammas Day, harvest happiness takes the place of midsummer madness. We gather our first harvest of wheat, but rather than bake it into loaves of bread, we weave it into a crown to be placed on our statue of Ceres.

Harvest Wreath

In September our gardens and nearby fields flaunt their brilliant colors. Blooms of yellow marigolds, orange calendulas, and bright goldenrods abound. Berries ripen, rose hips turn red, and the rowan (mountain ash) turns brilliant orange. With all this inspiration, we become so overwhelmed by the varying possibilities for harvest wreaths that we are apt to brush them all aside and do a simple circle of bearded Italian wheat. Most of our autumn wreaths, whether made from wild or garden materials or wheat imported from Italy, have the standard base of silver king artemisia, straw, or sweet Annie (*Artemisia annua*).

Marigolds and rose hips brighten a harvest wreath of bearded Italian wheat.

Simply push the stems of the marigolds and rose hips into the base.

In recent years miniature corn dollies have become popular decorations at Caprilands. Since they have a long history as a harvest symbol, we appropriately add them to wreaths made from various grains. We decorate with these wreaths in autumn, and they last until the Christmas season.

Witch's Wreath

The witch's wreath represents the many plants that both attract and repel witchcraft. It can hardly guarantee either purpose. Our intent is to call attention to the superstitions and beliefs surrounding these autumn plants.

Some essential plants to use in the composition of a witch's wreath are rue, cranesbill blossoms (wild geranium), willow, hawthorne, elder, alder, and rowan tree berries. It is written that rowan sticks were carried in the purses of many country people in England in the last century to protect them from evil spirits. You might also use dill, valerian, or vervain. Oak leaves may be added to this magical wreath, as the oak and the ash were used for and against witches; folklore authorities agree that they will either help or hinder the witch, depending upon their applications. Holly may also be used, for it reputedly is hated by witches. The leaves are reminiscent of the crown of thorns—the red berries, the blood of Christ. Bracken and ferns and some branches of yew or the yew berries add extra interest.

Oak leaves in a witch's wreath have a "special power."

A simple wreath of oak leaves surrounds a jack-o-lantern.

In the past, we have made many types of witch's wreaths using all these materials. The one we make today has a base of artemisia, also known as "ghost plant." In tipping the base we add a few pieces of wormwood (*Artemisia absinthium*). The seed heads of this plant, supposedly magical, are quite decorative in autumn. Around the edges of the wreath, we insert year-old artemisia curls, which have turned brown. Rowan tree berries come next in importance; they lend the autumn color and are an anathema to witches, for the color reminds them of the fires that consumed so many of their sisters. Then we insert the heads of dill, which according to legend, "hinders witches of their will." Blue-green sprigs of rue are next in order, and heads of tansy add a brilliant autumn yellow. After all this color has been added we surround it with the seed heads of the wild clematis (*Clematis virginiana*). This grows on old stone walls and looks like smoke in late

*Wild clematis looks like smoke on a wreath, but is not as fragile
as it appears.*

September and October. You can pick it in long vines, which can be
cut to size for wreath making. According to legend, wild clematis,
too, has magic; witches wrapped it around themselves to make them
fly. We have found that clematis lasts for a long time. It looks fragile
but actually clings together very well and does not shatter.

We make another type of witch's wreath from broom, which, of
course, is a very special witch's plant. Broom branches keep green and
can be intertwined with grapevines, eliminating the artemisia base.
We decorate the wreath with almost all of the varieties of plants
mentioned above. They can be inserted into the base without wiring.

Sometimes we simply make wreaths of wild Virgin's bower (*Clematis
vitalba*), also called traveler's joy. The pliable branches easily form a
circle. They make effective witch's crowns or can be used to decorate a
window or doorway.

Broom branches make a sturdy base for a witch's wreath.

What's more appropriate to add to a witch's wreath than a little witch?

Fall shades of strawflowers and goldenrod are attractive on an artemisia base.

St. Martin's Wreath

I recall St. Martin depicted on the stained glass windows of northern European churches. He sits on a prancing steed wearing a richly embroidered gold cape. According to legend, he took this cape, tore it down the middle, and gave half to a beggar to keep him from freezing. Out of this deed, St. Martin became known as the first of gift givers, preceding St. Nicholas.

St. Martin's Day falls on November 11 and is, appropriately, the first saint's day of the Christmas holiday season. In northern European countries, the great Christmas market opens on this day.

St. Martin's Day was also the time of the year that farmers slaughtered their livestock and salted the meat to eat during winter. It was customary to kill a "mart"—an ox so called because of St. Martin. In addition, the Martinmas Foy, a farm festival originally held on November 21 by the old calendar, was celebrated on November 11. It was the time for feasting and fond farewells when hired farm workers left for their homes or winter work.

Caprilands now opens its Christmas season on St. Martin's Day. We arrange our first Christmas decorations in the St. Martin's Room of the house. To suggest the market atmosphere of the northern countries, we use Swedish decorations made from straw. Apples, hung by threads, swing from the ceiling. Branches of yew cover the beamed ceiling, and wreaths made from braided straw and little sheaves of oats bound or bowed with red decorate the walls.

Our St. Martin's wreath begins with a circle of braided straw, wrapped with embroidered Swedish woven binding. We add sprigs of boxwood to give the wreath a holiday look and wire small lady apples into the straw base for color and to signify the harvest. A bow of boxwood finishes the design. A small primitive carving of a mounted rider placed in the wreath satisfies my memories of St. Martin depicted in the stained glass windows.

Suspend an apple from St. Martin's wreath for some holiday color. To do this, use a large needle to draw the ribbon through the apple. Then secure the ribbon to the bottom of the wreath.

Braided straw makes a base for a St. Martin's wreath.

Advent Wreath

The lighting of an Advent wreath is a traditional event of the Christmas season. It is made from evergreens, a symbol of hope. Four candles are placed in the wreath—one pink and three purple. The purple candles signify the penitential aspect of Advent, and the pink one is a symbol of joy for the coming of the Christ Child. You can also use white candles tied with pink and purple ribbons. Each Sunday during the four weeks of Advent a family member lights one of the candles and a prayer is said for family and friends. The lighted candles represent the Christ Child, the Light of the World. The pink one is lit on the fourth Sunday just preceding Christmas, known as Gaudete Sunday. *Gaudete* is the Latin for "rejoice."

The Advent wreath is our principal decoration for the Christmas season. The first wreath we designed contained a wide variety of plants associated with delightful legends of the holidays, but it was too large and cumbersome. Gradually we shaped it to a practical table size; however, still it measures nearly two feet across.

We make our wreath on a special Advent frame that has holders for the candles. This saves us much time and labor in construction. We bind a generous amount of sphagnum moss to the ring, so that once wet it will hold enough moisture for the living herbs that we will add. We cut branches of juniper with the frosty berries still on them, if possible, and force them into the frame to make a good circle. Juniper is called the plant of sanctuary, for it once sheltered the holy family. Also, it was used by St. Francis in the first creche at Greccio.

To the base we add symbolic herbs appropriate to the season. Bedstraw was in the manger with the hay and, according to a Spanish legend, its white flowers turned to gold with the Christ Child's radiance. Rosemary, dedicated to the Virgin Mary, turned its flowers to blue in Mary's honor. Pennyroyal reputedly bloomed at midnight when the Christmas bells rang. We use mints for wisdom, thyme for courage, sage for immortality, lavender for purity and virtue, and rue for good health and good fortune.

After the base is finished, we insert the candles. Sometimes we use the traditional purple candles with one pink one for Gaudete Sunday, but usually we use white. Around the candles we group dried purple and white statice. Occasionally, we add white globe amaranths, silver and purple sage, and silver cuttings of santolinas, which often root in the sphagnum moss. After all the herbs and flowers have been placed, we tie small bows of purple velvet around each of three of the candlesticks, and a pink one on the last candle.

Placed on a metal tray and watered, this Advent wreath will last through December and well into January.

Make an Advent wreath on a wire frame that will hold sphagnum moss. Frame should have holders for candles.

Right: Marigolds add bursts of brightness to a wreath of kitchen herbs.

The pale green female flowers of the twining hops plant make a distinctive wreath.

Keep a living wreath moist by spritzing it with water daily.

A wreath of lemon verbena dries to be useful.

A wreath of fresh bay laurel is beautiful by itself.

Mugwort and sweet fern make a Midsummer crown.

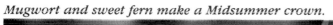

Friends gather for a pleasant afternoon wreath party at Caprilands.

Strawflowers and statice combine in a wedding decoration that will last for years.

Arrange daisies in concentric circles in a solid floral wreath.

Right: The heavy stalks of dill make a solid fragrant base.

Fresh herbs and flowers combine in a garland atop a gate.

Making a heart-shaped wreath is just as easy as making a round one. The key is to begin by bending heavy wire into the shape of a heart.

Shades of deep rose and purple predominate in a Victorian wreath.

A formal bouquet in wedding colors will dry and be attractive for years.

Traditional bridal herbs and flowers adorn the bride.

Bearded wheat alone makes a lovely wreath for a Lammas Day celebration.

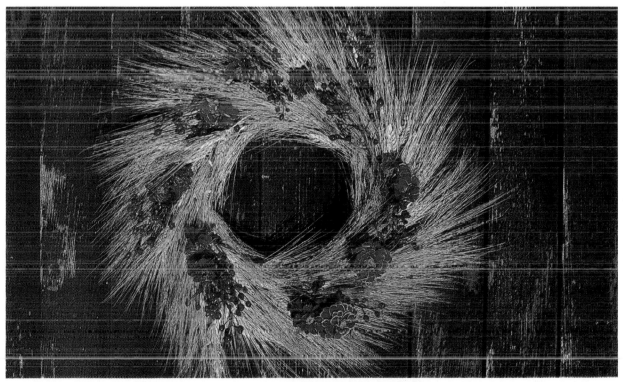

Decorate a fall wreath of bearded wheat with fresh or dried flowers.

Left: Seasonal wreaths adorn the Caprilands bookshop.

Grapevine and bittersweet combine to form the base of this autumn wreath.

The browns and golds of yarrow and goldenrod contrast with the base of artemisia.

Right: An artemisia base forms the support for fresh flowers and herbs.

Smoky-looking clematis highlights a witch's wreath.

A dried floral wreath can be made very full.

This full wreath is bursting with dried floral beauty.

A wreath of tansy and marigolds decorates an old wooden spinning wheel.

Goldenrod retains a lot of its color when dried, and makes a colorful wreath.

Small apples added to a St. Martin's wreath will remain attractive for several weeks.

Wheat and roses are the primary decorative elements on a St. Barbara's wreath.

Everlastings contrast with the pink of roses and the gold of wheat.

Cinnamon sticks are perfectly placed accents in this wreath.

A variety of herbal products are on display in the Caprilands shops.

Bows adorn many of the wreaths made at Caprilands.

Left: The workshop at Caprilands is both decorative and functional.

The white cardamom on an herb and spice wreath is a nice contrast to the red rose hips, rusty cinnamon, and silver artemisia.

The spikes on the brass frame of the St. Lucia's wreath hold the apples securely in place.

Lighting the Advent wreath is the traditional way to begin the Christmas season.

St. Barbara's Wreath

We made our first St. Barbara's wreath about 20 years ago. It was very simple, an unusual combination of wheat and roses. We designed it to represent the two principal symbols associated with this saint—bread and roses. Barbara, the daughter of a heathen family, was refused any contact with Christians. She spent much of her life as a prisoner in a tower, guarded by her father's soldiers. One day she was leaving the tower with bread from her kitchen to distribute among the poor. As she descended the steps, the guards stopped her. Her basket overturned, but instead of bread, roses spilled out.

The wheat used in a St. Barbara's wreath symbolizes not only the bread intended for the poor, but also the holy Eucharist, a reminder of her eventual conversion to Christianity.

To make a St. Barbara's wreath, we use a base of silver king artemisia and tip it with the finest end curls of the plant until we have a well balanced circle. Then we add a circle of dried rosebuds near the inside of the ring. The artemisia makes a good cushion for these fragile pink buds, which we select from our potpourri. We wire them in bunches or attach them with a glue gun for quicker handling. To add the wheat, we usually group three stems together and wire them into the wreath or simply push them in at intervals all around the wreath. Sometimes, we tie the wheat in a sheaf and attach it with the bow at the bottom. A large 14-inch St. Barbara's wreath makes a very handsome decoration for the mantle.

St. Barbara's wreath is a combination of wheat and roses.

For a festive holiday wreath place gray-green sage and bright red rose hips in a base of silvery artemisia.

St. Nicholas' Wreath

Our St. Nicholas' wreath may be made with either evergreens or artemisia. Sweet Annie *(Artemisia annua)* is a good choice, though, because its gold color is symbolic of the Dutch saint. Not only does it represent his gifts to the poor but also suggests the famous bags of gold he presented to the dowerless daughters of an impoverished nobleman to free them from slavery. At Caprilands, we like to add golden flowers, such as yarrow or tansy, to carry out this theme. They also suggest the gold pieces that the good children of Holland find in their shoes on Christmas morning.

St. Nicholas Day is also the time when beautiful cookie molds are used for the famous springerle, a German anise cake stamped with a wooden mold. You can find cookie molds in a variety of interesting shapes, and they make fine wreath decorations. We have some unusual metal ones that add brightness to our wreaths. We drill them and wire them to a green juniper background. To finish off the wreath we attach small bunches of spices, such as cinnamon sticks and nutmeg, which are commonly used to flavor the home-baked treats of the Christmas season.

Cookie cutters dangle
from a St. Nicholas' wreath.

St. Lucia's Wreath

St. Lucia is the patron saint of the eyes because she wore a crown of lighted candles on her head to represent the light of the world. In celebrating St. Lucia's Day, we bring out old brass wreaths that were originally Swedish Lucy crowns. They stand about three inches high

The lighted candles of the St. Lucia's wreath recall the crown of candles this saint wore.

and are very bright and shiny. They have holders for candles and sharp metal points to hold small lady apples or crab apples. We decorate the base with boxwood and rose hips and add small red velvet bows to give it a festive look. Last we place candles in the holders and light them for our celebration.

Ivy Wreaths

Ivy wreaths are a pleasure to make because ivy is so easy to train. To make our living ivy wreath, we take a planting frame and fill it with wet sphagnum moss. We place small ivy plants in the frame, burying the roots in the sphagnum and wiring the plants in place. The frame takes about eight ivies. They must be small to be inserted into the moss easily, but they will grow. We then fill the empty spaces with cuttings from our best ivy plants.

I like to decorate this wreath with white material. In our original design, we placed bunches of gray-white candleberries at even intervals around the wreath and attached a moss green velvet bow with a bit of white tied in. We've also made this wreath with touches of red, using holly berries from the wild native holly (*Ilex verticulata*) and finishing the design with a red bow.

Ivy is easy to train on a wreath planting frame.

If you hang the wreath outside on a door, it will hold the moisture for several days before additional water is needed, unless you live in an arid climate. Feel the wreath and when it is dry, take it down and water it well. To prevent it from harming the finish on your door, cover the back with plastic wrap or foil.

Use an ivy wreath to decoratively surround the punch bowl at your next party.

Miniature Wreaths

As the year winds down, we find we have a good collection of odds and ends of leftover materials, so we use them to make some small six-inch wreaths. For these miniature wreaths we begin with a base of sweet Annie about two inches thick. Using a glue gun to hold materials in place, we then dot the base with tiny pieces of tansy, amaranth, tiny strawflowers, and little bits of yarrow. These wreaths make delightful fragrant little gifts, or you can place them around candlesticks in table decorations.

Miniature wreaths make delightful gifts.

III

WREATH MATERIALS AND CONSTRUCTION

The first step in wreath construction is to obtain the materials. You should prepare and assemble more material than you think you will need, so that you will not have to halt progress on a wreath project to replenish supplies.

One way to be assured of having plenty of herbs is to grow your own. Planning and planting an herb garden can be a time of great pleasure if you approach it with a sense of adventure. Learn the histories and legends of the plants you grow, and you will experience some of the delights of the plant gatherers of the past. Designing an herb garden is an adventure in creativity. Be a gourmet and specialize in kitchen herbs. Be a perfumer and grow your own fragrances. Or be a plain dirt gardener and share the common kinship of all who cultivate the soil. Whatever your perspective, you will discover that many herbs are quite hardy and will grow even under trying conditions. You won't need the proverbial green thumb to grow most wreath materials successfully.

Combine materials in wreaths that you grow with those that you gather from the wild.

In addition to growing your own herbs and flowers, you can gather wild plants from the countryside to supplement the materials from your garden or even to provide all the flowers and foliage for a particular project. Ditches, pastures, and fallow fields are rich sources of wreath materials. You'll find enough to give you all the variety in color, texture, and size that you could want—plants that are lacy and delicate, as well as those that are bold and sturdy. In the fall, you can find many plants and seedpods that have dried in the fields and are ready for use.

Of course, you can also purchase wreath materials in craft stores, florist's shops, gift shops, and garden centers. You will find the freshest materials and the best prices in country markets and at flower shows. Consider also purchasing supplies through the mail. Check the advertisements in gardening and herb publications for addresses and catalog information.

Bittersweet is one vine that makes a good wreath base; it grows wild in the countryside.

German statice makes a light, delicate wreath base, left; thyme has a darker, heavier appearance.

Herbs for Wreath Bases

You will, of course, need material for the wreath base. A variety of plants exist that make nice backgrounds whether you are creating a delicate Victorian look, a homespun country design, or something more bold.

BROOM BRANCHES (*Cytisus* spp.) dry green and make attractive bases. Cut them after they blossom in late summer and form them immediately into the shapes required. Hang them until you are ready to decorate.

CLUB MOSSES or GROUND PINES (*Lycopodium* spp.) grow in the wild and do not dry well, so it is best to collect them the day you are going to use them. Store them in water in a cool, damp place out of the sun. Never keep them in sacks, for they will turn yellow. For house decorations, arrange them the day they are pulled and let them dry in place. They will keep their color, but they become quite fragile and cannot tolerate moving or trimming.

EVERGREENS create bold, fragrant backgrounds for Christmas wreaths. Branches should be cut just before you use them. Store them in water and keep them out of sunlight.

HONEYSUCKLE (*Aquilegia canadensis*) and GRAPEVINES (*Vitis* spp.) are popular base materials today. Curl your vines into wreaths as you cut them. Wire them if needed and hang them immediately because the vines stiffen quickly. You will need lots of storage space if you are making many wreaths from vines.

Since moss does not dry well, form it into a base as soon as possible after collecting it.

SILVER KING ARTEMISIA (*Artemisia ludoviciana* var. *albula*) is the variety of artemisia we use most often at Caprilands. The first grade is prime quality and shows no signs of damage. Hang it to dry until you are ready to use it. When you cut it for use, do not discard the plume-like tops or the many stems; they can be used in other decorations. Arrange them freely in decorative boxes or baskets and place them around your home where you can enjoy them until they are needed.

The second grade of silver king is material that has been abused in some way. It may have been harvested too early and consequently did not head properly, or it may have been weatherbeaten in a storm, had too little sun, or fallen to the ground in bunches. Keep it all. If some is

The curling tips of silvery artemisia make a distinctive wreath base.

muddy, wash and dry it outdoors in the sun; then hang it. Use the tips if you can, or bind the stems into bases. In the dead of winter, when you have little plant material left at all, it will look much better to you.

SILVER MOUND (*Artemisia schmidtiana* 'Nana') looks lovely in the garden, but it loses its soft texture with drying. It is worth mentioning, however, because it can be cut and saved for emergency use (padding or masking a base made of hay). Harvest it in late August, when it ceases to be attractive in the garden, and hang it to dry.

STRAW or FRESH-CUT HAY should be stored in burlap bags or plastic containers. Be sure the containers are airtight because any moisture will encourage mildew.

SWEET ANNIE (*Artemisia annua*) makes a fragrant base for all dried decorations. Cut it at different periods of growth. After it starts to mature in July, it changes in color and texture from light green to green with brown to almost white seeds by fall. With the frost it turns a rich brown and looks lovely in all kinds of fall creations. To grow sweet Annie in your garden, shake out the seeds from an old wreath over an area where you would like to grow this herb. The next spring the seeds will germinate into soft green seedlings. Sweet Annie grows quickly and will soon be six feet tall. After harvesting it, hang the entire plant from a wire or cut off the branches and hang them in bunches.

Herbs for Color

The herbs and flowers listed here are excellent sources of color for wreaths, whether fresh or dried. It is a fortunate wreath-maker who has a good supply of these on hand. You'll find in this list some good sources of blue, a color difficult to find among herbs.

ALLIUMS (*Allium* spp.) are plants of the onion family. They produce interesting seed heads, which dry well. The flowers of these ornamental onions range from pale mauve to white. Their strong stems can be inserted directly into the base of many wreaths.

ANGELICA (*Angelica archangelica*) produces spectacular globe-shaped clusters of yellow-green or white-green blossoms and large seed heads that dry beautifully. Use them in large wreaths or attach them in place of a bow on a finished wreath.

Bachelor's buttons make delightful additions to dried herb and flower wreaths.

BACHELOR'S BUTTONS (*Centaurea cyanus*), especially blue ones, should be harvested just as they are coming into full bloom. Hang them to dry, and then pack them carefully in boxes to store; they are very fragile.

CELOSIA (*Celosia* spp.) has a strong red color, which is hard to find in plants that can be dried easily without the use of sand, borax, or silica gel. Cut celosia in its prime and hang it to dry away from strong light.

Plumelike celosias provide feathery accents for wreaths.

DELPHINIUMS (*Delphinium* spp.) come in wonderful shades of blue. They should be cut when not quite in full blossom and hung singly to dry. Treasure every bit of these flowers; if any break into fascicles (clusters of flowers or leaves), use a glue gun to attach them to your wreath.

GOLDENROD (*Solidago* spp.) as its name implies, is an excellent source of golden yellow flowers. Many varieties exist. Harvest the flowers early in their fall blooming. You can hang them to dry, or weave them directly into a wreath. At Caprilands we use the lance leaf goldenrod (*Solidago graminifolia*), the earliest to bloom in the garden, as part of the background in our wreaths.

HIGHBUSH CRANBERRY (*Viburnum trilobum*) belongs to the honeysuckle family and is a good source of dark red berries, although they give off an unpleasant odor when crushed. They keep a long time in water.

NIGELLA (*Nigella damascena*) produces interesting seed pods in greens and browns, sometimes streaked with purple. The frilly foliage adds a wispy texture to wreaths. Gather stems when the pods have started to open at the top.

The balloonlike seed pods of nigella are fun to use in wreaths.

SAFFLOWER (*Carthamus tinctorius*) dries nicely and offers bright warm oranges. Its spiky leaves bring interesting texture to wreaths. Cut stems when some of the flowers are fully open and others are still in bud. Hang them in bunches to dry.

SALVIA (*Salvia farinacea*) produces one of the best blues in the herb garden, bluer than most lavenders. Hang them to dry and pack them carefully when storing.

The orange blossoms of safflower dry nicely.

STATICE (*Limonium* spp.) in pink, lavender, and yellow is commonly sold in bunches. Although you can start it from seed, we have found it difficult to grow in the dry stony soil at Caprilands. Hang it in bunches to store. It is very durable and good for outside wreaths as it revives in a rain.

STRAWFLOWERS (*Helichrysum bracteatum*) have very fragile stems that need wiring. Harvest while the centers of the flowers are still tight, and attach wires to the heads to give support to the stems. Strawflowers are an excellent source of gold and rust colors.

TANSY (*Tanacetum vulgare*) can be cut at different stages, but if picked too soon it will shrivel. Young plants dry to yellow; mature plants dry to light brown.

YARROW (*Achillea millefolium*) comes in yellow, pink, white, and even dark red varieties. One of the white yarrows looks like little roses. All dry well if hung in small bunches. The strong stems do not require wiring. If a flower head seems too large for an arrangement, it can be broken into small segments and then attached to the wreath.

Buttonlike tansy blossoms can brighten any herb and flower wreath.

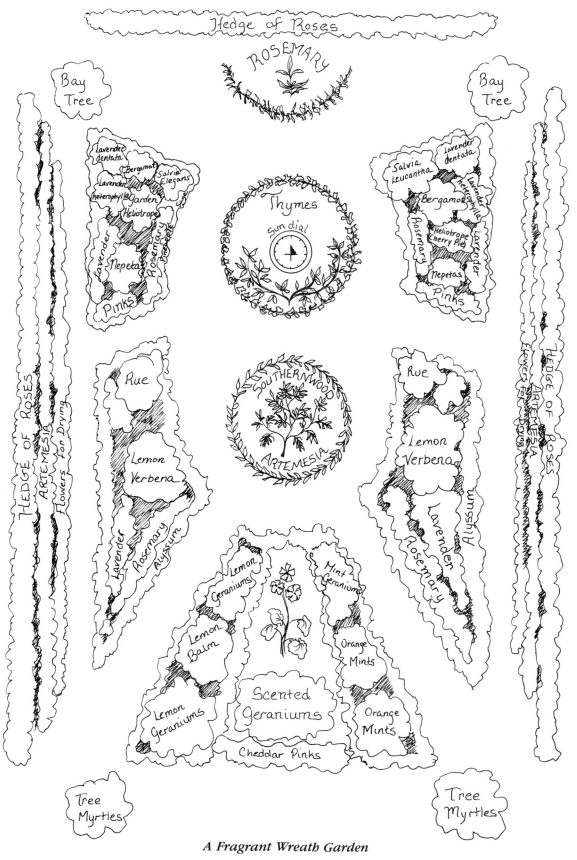

A Fragrant Wreath Garden

Herbs for Fragrance

A garden of fragrant herbs may seem unnecessary, for all herbs have some fragrance. Certain herbs, however, have special distinctive scents to warrant making a separate fragrance garden. One of the prime reasons for planting a fragrance garden at Caprilands was to supply the ingredients for our potpourris, rose jars, sweet pillows, sachets, and sweet-smelling wreaths. Most of these have a base of either roses or lavender.

Hedges of roses border the Caprilands fragrance garden. These are the taller bush varieties that need space and full sun—damask, centifolia, Lancaster, York, Austrian copper, Harrison's yellow, and old moss roses. Inside the tall rose bushes, we have planted artemisia and flowers for drying. At the four corners stand bay and myrtle trees. We surrounded the raised beds with board siding. Fieldstone walks separate the individual plantings, and grey granite-chip walks outline the garden.

We designed the largest bed in the shape of a fan and divided it into three sections. On one side we grow the pungent mints, mint geraniums, and sweet orange mint.

The center section is devoted to a few of our favorite scented geraniums. We grow the three kinds of rose-scented geraniums: the old-fashioned rose geranium (*Pelargonium graveolens*), Robert's lemon rose, and the skeleton rose. These geraniums are natives of South Africa; their fragrance is sweeter than roses and lasts much longer. Along the borders of this section we grow spicy-scented cheddar pinks (*Dianthus gratiano politanus*), the velvety mint geranium, the low-growing nutmeg-scented geranium, apple-scented geraniums, and old spice geraniums. All scented geraniums give off their fragrance only when brushed or crushed and smell even sweeter when dried.

Lemon balm spreads through the adjoining section. We dry this for potpourris and recommend it to all who enjoy a lemon scent. Lemon geraniums also grow here. They look like little trees with curled leaves, and they release a sweet citrus odor when brushed. Their crisp leaves and stout stems retain their shape when dried and are excellent for wreath making.

In the center of the garden, we planted a lemon-scented southernwood (*Artemisia arbrotanum*) bush. Its foliage adds a spicy scent to our herbal wreaths.

Our most fragrant thymes grow around a small sundial placed on a decorative stone in a round bed. These include golden lemon, narrowleaf French, grey and silver culinary thymes, creeping golden lemon, green lemon, and spicy-smelling thymes. We use them fresh and dried in our kitchen wreaths.

A bay tree marks the corner of the fragrance garden.

Another bed in the fragrance garden contains a gigantic potted rosemary *(Rosmarinus officinalis)* which we bring indoors for winter. We surrounded this bush with small plants of creeping rosemary *(Rosmarinus prostratus)*. They make an excellent ground cover and blossom frequently. We cut sprigs from these plants to use in our herb and spice wreaths.

In beds on each side of the thyme we planted hardy lavenders. We combine cuttings from these plants with rosemary and sage in wedding wreaths. Included among our lavenders is a stunning *Lavandula heterophylla* bush. It blooms almost continuously and has sweet-smelling foliage, even when dried. Though hardy, it must be wintered inside. We grow tender *L. dentata* also for its sweet foliage.

Lavenders are among the most important sources of fragrance.

In early spring, we set lemon verbenas into two narrow beds. When planted, they look like pitiful little sticks, but before summer's end, they become attractive shrubs with hundreds of lemon-scented leaves. Natives of the high mountains of Guatemala, Mexico, and South America, they grow best in very warm weather. In our region, lemon verbenas must be wintered inside. They bitterly resent change and drop their leaves when moved. Lemon verbenas add a wonderful fragrance to any type of fragrant wreath. A tasty tea can be brewed from the leaves of lemon verbena, making it a good choice for a tea wreath.

A variety of good plants for
wreaths grow in the borders
of the fragrance garden.
Artemisia, bottom left, and
hyssop, right, can be used
fresh or dried. Dahlias, top
left, and asters, below, are
best when used fresh.

The two back beds in the fragrance garden contain our pinks. The carnation types are called "sops in wine" because they were once added to drinks. They are a good source of scent and color in early summer. This bed is also home to our bergamots, one red and one very pale pink, which furnish us with scented leaves all season long. They bloom in late summer. Bergamot is another plant from which you can make a citrusy tea. For this reason, we use both the leaves and flowers to make wreaths for tea tables.

In the fall, these same beds are ablaze with color from the salvias—*Salvia elegans*, with its long red spikes of blossoms, and *S. leucantha*, with its velvety purple blooms. Both these sages are fragrant, although many do not find the scent of *S. leucantha* entirely pleasant. We use both of these salvias in wedding and kitchen wreaths.

Rosemary makes an elegant and very fragrant wreath that would delight a gourmet cook.

Combine leaves from several lemon-scented plants into an attractive wreath.

Lemon verbena has a delightful fragrance, both fresh and dried.

~ Making Potpourris for Wreaths ~

You can take cuttings from any of the plants described above and add them directly to wreaths for fragrance, but another way to bring scent to a wreath is by attaching small sachets or bags of potpourri. Many of the Capriland designs use sachets of potpourri as decorative elements. Following are some pleasing recipes for potpourris that will bring fragrance into your home during winter, long after the scented blossoms of your garden have faded.

Garden Potpourri

1 quart dried rose geranium
    leaves
1 quart dried lemon balm leaves
1 quart dried lavender leaves
1 cup dried thyme
1 cup dried apple mint leaves
1 cup dried sweet marjoram
1 cup dried lemon thyme
1 quart dried rosebuds
¼ cup powdered cloves
1 cup granulated orrisroot
2 drops musk oil

Mix all the ingredients thoroughly in a large bowl. Store in covered containers for at least two weeks so that fragrances blend.

Small bags of garden potpourri can be attached to wedding wreaths, crowns, or tussie mussies.

Sweet Woodruff Potpourri

Sweet woodruff is most fragrant when dry. In the past, it was used to drive away moths and to scent rooms. Like rose geraniums, it can be used alone without fixatives; however, for longer lasting fragrance mix in a pinch of orrisroot and a ground vanilla bean.

Lavender Potpourri

This recipe may be used in sachets or as the base for a spice potpourri.

1 pound dried lavender flowers
¼ pound gum benzoin
¼ pound granulated orrisroot
¼ ounce oil of lavender

Grind the lavender flowers and gum benzoin into a fine powder and place in a large bowl.

Mix together the orrisroot and lavender oil and combine with the lavender.

Sewn into sachets, this potpourri adds a lovely fragrance to wedding wreaths.

(continued)

Making Potpourris for Wreaths—*Continued*

Herb Potpourri

This recipe is an excellent way to use the overflow harvest of your herb garden, as well as bits and pieces of plants left over from wreath making. Its refreshing scent is not as sweet as most potpourris.

1 cup dried rosemary
2 cups dried thyme
4 cups dried lemon verbena leaves
4 cups dried lemon balm leaves
1 cup dried sweet marjoram
1 cup dried orange mint leaves
2 cinnamon sticks
¼ pound cloves
½ pound allspice
1 pound dried rose petals
½ pound dried lavender flowers
¼ pound granulated orrisroot
½ cup granulated orrisroot
1 ounce rose oil

Using a mortar and pestle or a blender, coarsely crush the rosemary, thyme, lemon verbena, lemon balm, marjoram, orange mint, and cinnamon sticks and set aside.

Grind the cloves and allspice and mix them together. In a large bowl, combine the herbs, spices, and rose and lavender petals. Add the ¼ pound of orrisroot and mix well.

Store the potpourri in a tightly covered jar for about one month. Before using, add ½ cup orrisroot blended with 1 ounce rose oil and mix in thoroughly. Small bags or sachets filled with this potpourri can be added to the design of a wreath or attached under the bow.

Orange Potpourri

We make this potpourri after our holiday entertaining, when we have an accumulation of unused lemon, lime, and orange peels, after the fruits for our festive punches have been juiced.

To prepare citrus peels for potpourri, scrape away the pulp and membrane to prevent mold from growing later. Then cut the peels into strips, place them in a wire basket and dry them over a warm stove or in a slow oven. Stir the peels frequently to aid drying. When the peels are crackle-dry, crush them to a powder using a grinder, a mortar and pestle, or even a rolling pin.

2 cups ground citrus peels, predominantly orange
1 quart dried orange blossoms
dried orange calendula and orange marigold blossoms, enough for color
1 quart dried orange mint and pineapple mint leaves
1 cup granulated orrisroot
20 drops orange blossom oil
10 drops oil of bergamot

Combine all the ingredients in a large bowl. Transfer the mixture to a tightly covered container and allow it to set for at least a week before using.

Put this potpourri into tiny lace or silk bags and tie into an orange-blossom wedding wreath.

Wedding Potpourri

This is the simplest of all potpourris. It will remain sweet and fragrant in an open bowl for several months. For a longer-lasting fragrance, add granulated orrisroot and the essence of rosemary and lemon verbena to the mixture. For color, add dried bachelor's buttons, pinks, and peony petals.

4 cups fresh rosemary clippings
2 cups fresh lemon verbena leaves
4 cinnamon sticks, ground
¼ cup ground cloves

Combine all ingredients in a large bowl, or sew tiny sachets and tie onto a wedding wreath.

Rose Geranium Potpourri

Prolific rose geraniums can be harvested throughout the summer or cut in large masses at the season's end. Hang them to dry in an airy room, away from direct sunlight. They dry very quickly. Then remove the leaves from the stems. A single geranium easily produces enough foliage for more than a quart of dried leaves. The best varieties for rose geranium potpourri are Robert's lemon rose, the sweetest of the rose scents; skeleton rose; and the familiar *Pelargonium graveolens*. A rose geranium potpourri does not need essences and fixatives, although the leaves do have to be crushed to emit a strong scent.

Gathering Herbs and Flowers for Wreaths

I feel at times a love and joy
For every weed and everything
A feeling kindred, from a boy
A feeling brought with every spring.
                              —John Clare

Every gardener delights in all green and growing things while, at the same time, resents days spent ridding garden plots of weeds. However, when we take a closer look at weeds, we find that many of them are beautifully formed. At Caprilands we welcome a few "weeds" into our garden. Goldenrods seed everywhere and, of course, must be controlled, but we do let a few grow in special places. The lance leaf, which blooms every year, is a special favorite of ours.

Dock, too, springs up in many places, and we usually leave a few plants to bloom. This spreads so rapidly that it must be carefully watched, or the herb garden will look like a weed plot.

Wildflowers and grasses combine in a delightful seasonal decoration.

The field daisy (*Chrysanthemum leucanthemum*) and St.-John's-wort (*Hypericum perforatum*) also spread into cultivated beds. We permit the daisies to remain until they get rampant, but we never have enough St.-John's-wort. We must rely on a nearby meadow to supply the large quantities we use.

Gather fresh violets and their leaves in the springtime to create a miniature wreath.

The perennial aster is allowed more space in our garden than any other wild plant. We like to use the blossoms of many varieties in our fall decorations. Milkweed springs up near sheds and outbuildings, and we use this plant in fall decorations, too. The grey rosettes of mullein leaves make interesting accents in summer and autumn gardens; we grow the green-leafed, the cultivated silver Artic snow, and the wooly white flannel plant (*Verbascum thapsus*).

A wreath made from one variety of grass looks best when full.

But we don't limit our weed gathering to the garden. Each year in late June, as soon as the hay and field grains start to grow, we wander into the shaggy pastures filled with wild growth. There we find colonies of Queen Anne's lace, the early goldenrod, the false oats, and the broom grass. Feathery June grass, red-top Timothy, and a wealth of small flowers mingle there, too. Many of the grasses retain their color if picked green and dried quickly. The summer months at Caprilands are often so busy that harvesting them early is almost impossible. As a result, we pick these treasures in late August and early September when they have turned brown or shades of tan. Combined with seedpods and autumn flowers, they make delightful decorations, especially when placed against wood paneled backgrounds and on mantels.

The following wild plants are the most popular ones used in our wreaths. They grow plentifully in fields and along roadsides.

AMARANTH *(Amaranthus retroflexus)* is a thick, tall, and hearty plant, which produces its flowers in panicles at the top of the stem. It dries well and can be cut to size and shaped into patterns for autumn wreaths and swags.

ASH *(Fraxinus americana)* produces interesting keys, or seedpods.

BARBERRY *(Berberis vulgaris)* displays bright red berries in fall, and its foliage turns red, also. Branches of this shrub can be added to wreaths to give a splash of color.

BAYBERRY *(Myrica pensylvanica)* is grey-white in color. Cuttings add interest to a greyish wild wreath.

BITTERSWEET *(Celastrus scandens)* should be cut as soon as the leaves drop and the fruit turns yellow. Usually they are ready in late August or early September. Collect branches when the berries have their yellow husks still on and before they open; do not wait for frost. Bring the branches indoors and hang them overnight. The yellow pods will open and expose the beautiful orange-red fruit. Harvested this way, the outer yellow shell will not drop off. Bittersweet belongs to the poisonous nightshade family, so do not use its fruit or leaves for anything but decorations.

BONESET *(Eupatorium perfoliatum)* was once used to make a tea for colds and fevers. The blossoms of this herb turn a yellowish white with drying and make excellent additions to floral arrangements.

Shaggy seed heads and seed pods are abundant along roadsides and in fields in late summer and fall.

Globe thistle has a small round seed head.

DOCK (*Rumex* spp.) is a common weed in several varieties, all of which dry reasonably well. This plant can be harvested from the green stage on through its darkest and driest period. If cut early in the season, the tall seed heads will dry to green. A little later, they will have a red or pink cast, and if left until late October or November, they will dry to a deep brown. If you have space in your backyard, grow enough dock so that it can be harvested at these different stages. We grow ours near the barn, where it is quite at home. In neglected pastures pick dock early in the season because farmers dislike it and remove it quickly. When adding dock to wreaths, do not try to use the flowering stalk whole but break it into segments for easy insertion.

Dock seed heads may dry in shades of green, red, or brown, depending on when they are picked.

ELDER *(Sambucus canadensis)* is a shrub that can grow to 15 or 20 feet tall; however it usually takes on a broad and spreading form. Five smaller varieties are generally known, and there are several cultivars. Branches of elderberry look lovely in autumn bouquets and wreaths. We also use the tree boughs and fruits in the witch's wreath.

GOLDENROD *(Solidago* spp.) is a perennial herb common in fields. At least a hundred varieties of this prolific plant exist. You can cut it from late July through August and into October. The lance leaf, *Solidago graminifolia,* must be harvested early—as soon as the flowers turn yellow—or the blooms will blast and turn to fluff. You can add them fresh to wreaths and let them dry in the design, or you can hang them to dry and add them later. Pick most varieties before the gold is fully developed and dry them in the dark. Some may discolor, but much should be usable. We use goldenrods lavishly in our wreaths, and we never seem to cut enough.

HAZEL or HAZELNUT *(Corylus americana)* is a hardy deciduous tree or shrub native to North America, cultivated for its edible nuts. It is often called cobnut or filbert and the nuts work nicely into autumn wreath designs with pine cones and grasses. The leaves of many species are very colorful in fall, and golden yellow male catkins are attractive in the spring.

The fruit of the hops plant looks like little lanterns.

HOPS *(Humulus lupulus)* produces a fruit that resembles a little Japanese lantern. This fruit dries very well but shatters easily, so handle it with care. Cut it as soon as it is well developed. We make autumn wreaths of hop blossoms. They also look nice simply hung in a window above our punch bowl.

GROUND IVY *(Glechoma hederacea)* is related to catnip and has been used in medicinal teas and as a flavoring for homemade ale. At Caprilands we call it by one of its old names—Jill over the ground or ale hoof. It produces pretty small blue blossoms. We have planted it as a ground cover under trees where little else will grow. It can be twined around a wreath gracefully and has a slightly medicinal fragrance.

JOE-PYE WEED *(Eupatorium maculatum)* is named after an Indian who treated fevers with this plant. You will usually be able to find it in wet meadows, swamps, and beside lakes and streams. The lovely thick pink heads must be picked practically in bud stage, or they will turn brown on drying or burst into fluff and be useless. Blossoms start to show in the fields in late July, August, and September. Rarely does an entire flower head open and dry evenly, so we often rip out the discolored sections and use only the part that has dried to a good pink.

JUNIPER *(Juniperus sabina)* is a low-growing evergreen that thrives in sterile, rocky soil and spreads rapidly in neglected pastures. The name means "forever young." Of all our native trees, we use the juniper most often in wreath making. Its greens last a very long time. We make the bases for our Advent wreaths and living arrangements from juniper, and it is the principal greenery used in our Christmas decorations.

KNOTWEED *(Polygonum spp.)* includes a huge family of invasive plants. Some species have small pink blossoms, and others have white ones. Used fresh, they add color and brightness to living wreaths. They also dry well.

MILKWEED *(Asclepias syriaca)* produces pods that add a lot of interest to wreaths and herb decorations. We prefer to use them in their natural colors—grey-browns with creamy insides. However, they can be painted or gilded for certain projects.

MULLEIN *(Verbascum thapsus)* was known in the past as flannel plant, baby Jesus's flannel, Virgin's candlestick, and hag's taper. It is probably the most spectacular of the common weeds. Both the leaves, pressed and dried, and the blossoms, broken into small sprigs, may be used in wreaths. In addition to the yellow wild mullein, many cultivated varieties are available with pink, purple, or white blossoms.

PEPPERGRASS, or field cresses (*Lepidium* spp.) can be collected from June to October. Picked green, these wild grasses keep their pale green color when dried. You can hang them to dry and use later or make a wreath with them upon harvesting. They will dry nicely in the wreath, giving it a light, feathery touch. Peppergrass works well in many designs, lending a dainty look when used as fillers in wreaths and bouquets. If your design suggests a brown grass, gather this plant in late fall.

QUEEN ANNE'S LACE *(Daucus carota)* is a handsome weed; its flat white flower heads truly resemble lace. Use them in very delicate wreath designs or in Christmas tree decorations.

ROSES (*Rosa* spp.) can be found growing in the wild as well as in the garden. The hedge rose, or multiflora rose, *Rosa chinensis*, forms a living fence and furnishes one of the best Christmas decorations, the rose hip. Rose hips may be harvested early, when still green, or after the frost, when they have turned red.

The beach rose, *Rosa rugosa*, is a very vigorous rose, with rough foliage and single blossoms. Its rose hips are very large seed cases that resemble small tomatoes. They add a bright splash of color to decorations and look quite handsome in wreaths; however, they do not last as long as the hips of the multiflora rose.

ST.-JOHN'S-WORT *(Hypericum perforatum)* looks quite brown and has perforated leaves. If left alone in a sunny location, this wort will take over a neglected pasture and will be ready for harvesting in early fall. It blooms about the time of St. John's Day, June 24, hence its name. By late summer, its yellow blossoms are replaced with red-brown seed heads, which make lovely dark accents in our wreath designs.

SMOOTH SUMAC *(Rhus glabra)* adds to wreaths a distinctive red color that is hard to find elsewhere. The fruit is too heavy to use all in one cluster. Break it up into small bits and place a wire around the part to be inserted into the wreath.

SPICEBUSH *(Lindera benzoin)* was once treasured by the Indians and the colonists. The bark has a fragrant and slightly spicy odor. It produces lovely yellow blossoms in the very early spring before its leaves appear. In the fall, its foliage turns golden and its fruits red.

SPIREA (*Spiraea* spp.) is a shrub that grows in damp meadows and pastures. Most species have white blossoms. Steeple top *Spiraea tomentosa* produces pink flowers that bloom on a short raceme and dry very well for use in wreaths and other decorations.

Both the bark and leaves of spicebush are used for fragrance The yellow flower blooms in early spring.

STAGHORN SUMAC *(Rhus typhina)* grows into a tall tree. We harvest its large velvety blossoms and break them into pieces for wreath decorations where red accents are needed.

SWEET EVERLASTING *(Gnaphalium* spp.) is a perennial that self sows in gardens but grows best in sandy, dry, neglected roadside areas. Harvest the mature plants in fall, from August to November, when they will be covered with a fine fluff. Shake the fluff from the plant to uncover a daisylike flower. We use a lot of everlasting in Caprilands creations.

Teasel may be grown in the garden or collected in the wild.

TEASEL (*Dipsacus sylvestris*) is a hardy biennial, but it sheds so many seeds that a new supply of plants comes up year after year if it likes its location. A tall prickly plant, its leaves meet in pairs at the stem to form a basin where water collects. From this, the plant became known as Virgin's basin. We grow it in the back of our largest garden and in our Saints' Garden. Its flowers are very small and purple and are replaced by seed heads that dry brown. These seed heads make fine accents in all kinds of herb decorations, wild grass wreaths, and herb and flower arrangements. It can be picked dry in the wild and does not need any further treatment.

WILD CLEMATIS (*Clematis virginiana*) has many decorative uses. Its long ropes of grey-green, feathery fluff trail along old stone walls and roadsides. Gather it when the white of the beard begins to show. It dries well and will not lose its fluff. Use it in witch's wreaths, twine it around grapevine wreaths, or drape it over windows and mantels. It will last indefinitely.

WILD HOLLY (*Ilex verticillata*) is a small tree, also known as black alder or winter berry, which grows in acid soil in swampy places. Its gorgeous scarlet winter berries last a long time and look stunning in Christmas wreaths.

WITCH HAZEL *(Hamamelis virginiana)* is a wild shrub that sometimes grows to 25 feet. Its yellow flowers bloom in October and early November after the leaves have fallen. The hard-shelled pods shoot out their seeds like bullets from a gun. To harvest, cut the flowers with long stems. They dry well in interesting forms for winter bouquets. The shelled seedpods make nice accents in wreaths.

YARROW *(Achillea millefolium)* grows pervasively in open fields. Hang it to dry, or use it fresh in wreaths.

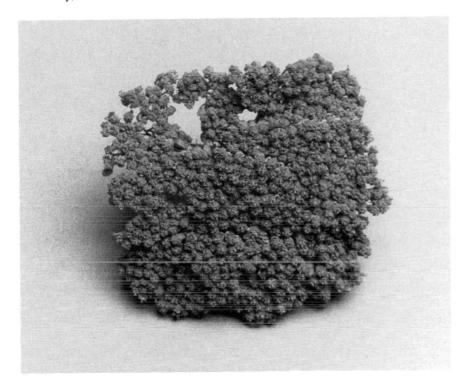

Yarrow can be gathered from open fields, and it dries nicely for use in wreaths.

Other plants that we gather from the wild to use in our wreaths include:

CANADA BLUEGRASS *(Poa compressa)*
HAIRYCRESS *(Bromus commutatus)*
JAPANESE WITCH HAZEL *(Hamamelis japonica)*
OATS *(Avena sativa)*
SHEPHERD'S PURSE *(Capsella bursa-pastoris)*
SWEET VERNAL GRASS *(Anthoxanthum odoratum)*
TIMOTHY *(Phleum pratense)*
WITCHGRASS *(Panicum capillare)*

With such a variety of plants to grow and gather, all kinds of textures and color combinations can be created in your fresh and dried decorations.

Harvest and Preservation

The best time to pick material for wreath making is late morning. By that time, the sun has dried the dew but hasn't leached out the colors or the essential oils that keep perfumes intact and leaves and petals looking fresh.

Flower color is brightest when blooms first open. Many flowers will continue opening after they have been cut, so make allowance for this. Some flowers should be checked every day. For example, if strawflowers have been open too long, the centers turn to fluff. When harvesting flowers, follow this general rule: cut flowers when they are fully formed but the centers are still tightly closed. With experience, you will learn the best harvest times for each plant you use. When harvesting plants you are unfamiliar with, experiment to determine the optimum time for picking and drying.

Some herbs work best as wreath decorations when used directly from the garden or field. When fresh, they are still pliable enough to conform to the wreath shape. Grapevines should be stripped of leaves as soon as they are picked and then formed immediately into wreath bases. Likewise, broom branches should be shaped into wreaths while they are still pliable. Follow this practice with all heavy-stemmed plants gathered for wreath bases, including willow, bittersweet, and honeysuckle.

You will use certain herbs and flowers right away to make living wreaths. Others can be inserted fresh into arrangements and left to dry, but most of the materials you will use in wreaths and garlands will have to be dried or preserved in some way.

Many plants lose a lot of their bulk as they dry—above, cockscomb celosia grows plush and velvety; at left, it is dried and still a wonderful source of texture and color.

Plants dry best in a dark, well-ventilated space.

Hanging Herbs to Dry

The importance of a dry, dark, well-ventilated room for drying both foliage and flowers cannot be too strongly emphasized. Sun leaches the color out of many fine materials, and dampness causes mold and mildew.

A room with wooden walls works best because the wood absorbs moisture. Attics, lofts, balconies, garages, or other high places with good air circulation make ideal drying areas. Kitchens, if not too steamy or sunny, can also be used. Sheds open on one side are excellent sites for drying artemisias, as long as you are not expecting a long period of damp weather and you don't hang the artemisias too close together. Avoid hanging plants in dark closets; air does not circulate in them, and mold may develop on your plants. Do not try to dry or store wreath materials in a cellar unless you have prepared a warm, dry area. I don't recommend oven drying either; it makes materials very brittle.

A "bunch" for drying purposes means just a few stems. Top: Silver king artemisia; bottom: German statice.

Tie herbs and flowers in loose bunches to dry.

Flowers drop pieces as they dry, and the bundles may need to be retied.

In the early days at Caprilands, we dried our culinary herbs in the kitchen. This room has pine paneling and small windows. Air circulates well; little sun enters through the windows; and heat is constant. We also hung materials in an adjoining shed that is very deep, warm, and airy. At one time, before other areas became available, we dried flowers, particularly roses, in an unused upstairs bedroom. It was a sunny room, however, so we had to close the curtains to keep the roses from fading.

As the years passed, our original drying shed at Caprilands began to fill too quickly with the harvest of herbs, fragrant potpourri, and all kinds of dried floral decorations. Now we dry and preserve all our materials in the large lofts of the 18th century barn and in a new barn by our Identification Garden. We prefer air drying over any other method.

Many herbs can be dried by hanging in bunches. If you won't be using the leaves, strip them from the stems; they are a source of moisture, which encourages mold. Tie the stems together in loose bunches, so that air circulates among them. Experiment with sizes of bunches to determine the best one for each type of plant. Bunches that are too large tend to mold. As plants dry, the stems shrivel, and some will drop from the bunch; simply gather them up and retie them into the group. Hung from rafters, a pole, or a rack, the drying herbs are decorative. If you are not planning to use the dried material immediately, protect it from dust as well as light. Wrap hanging bushes loosely in paper or store dried material gently in spacious boxes.

Globe amaranth growing in a garden.

Globe amaranth gathered and dried.

Some flowers dry best on trays or screens.

Large stems that will be used to make wreath bases are often best dried in baskets. The stems of artemisias dry straight and very stiff when they are hung, but placed loosely in baskets when stems are fresh and pliable, they will droop over the edge as they dry and bend into gently curling shapes. They are then much easier to fashion into wreaths.

Rosebuds and other flowers that will be wired dry well in a single layer on trays or screens. Place these screens away from light in an airy spot. Decorative seedpods harvested from the garden or the fields can also be dried in this manner if they are not already thoroughly dry when you gather them. To dry Queen Anne's lace and other flowers with flat blossoms, puncture holes in the top of a box; then thread the stems through the holes so the flower heads rest on the lid. Place the lid back on the box.

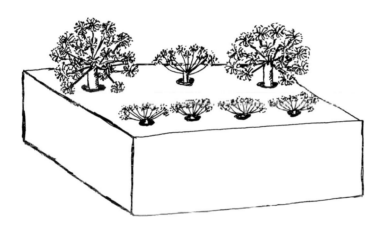

Insert stems of flowers with flat umbrels in a box to hold them as they dry.

In autumn, fields, roadsides, and ditches abound with material that can be picked and used in wreaths or bouquets just as it is. Don't ignore dried mushrooms or other types of fungi and unusual bits of weathered wood. These add interest to wild wreaths or an eerie touch to a witch's wreath. Drill them and wire them to your decoration or attach them with glue.

Drying Herbs

Many flowers dry best when placed in a drying medium, such as sand, borax, or silica gel. When this method was first discovered, sand was used, and it still works well today. If you choose to use sand, first wash it in buckets until it is perfectly clean. Then drain the water, and dry the sand thoroughly in heat, sun, or an oven.

Borax and silica gel also make good drying mediums. Silica gel is a commercial product that can be found in drugstores, craft stores, and florist's shops.

Directions for using silica gel appear on the box; however, all these drying agents are used in basically the same way. Simply follow these steps:

1. Spread a thin layer of the drying medium over the bottom of a wide, shallow container. At Caprilands we use tin containers and cake boxes for smaller flowers. They are airtight and easy to move without damaging the material. Heavy cardboard boxes work well for large flowers with long stems.

2. Place the flowers in the powder so that the blossoms don't touch.

Place flowers in silica gel so that they do not touch.

3. Gently pour the drying powder over and around the flowers until they are completely buried.

4. If using sand and borax, leave the container open. If using silica gel, the container must be sealed tightly.

5. Leave the containers to stand. In a warm, dry room the material will dry in three days to one week.

6. Lift the dried flowers very carefully from the medium, and use a soft brush to clean away any granules caught in the petals.

Flowers that have been dried in silica gel keep their form well.

Zinnias, marigolds, calendulas, and flowers with double petals, such as roses and violets, dry best using this method.

Preserving Herbs

Certain plants do not dry well at all and need to be treated with a preservative. Infusing a glycerine solution into leaves and berries preserves their natural color and texture. When using this technique, choose a location where your plant material can be kept in containers of liquid and undisturbed for a long period of time. To prepare the plants, first remove all damaged leaves or those that have blemishes; then scrape off the bark and split the ends of the woody stems about two to three inches. To infuse them with glycerine follow these steps:

1. Combine one part glycerine with two parts of very hot water. Pour the liquid into a bottle, cork tightly, and shake well until the glycerin and water are thoroughly mixed.

To preserve plants in glycerine, first choose a container that will support the stems, and will permit the liquid to rise two inches up the stems.

2. Pour the mixture into a container of a size that will hold the plants you are treating. For sprays of oak or beech, use an earthenware or stoneware jug; for single leaves, old cups or mugs work well.

3. Stand the stems in the glycerine solution. The liquid should be at a level of about two inches up the stems of the plant.

4. In a few days, check the level of the solution. If all of it has been absorbed, pour in more hot solution until it reaches the original level.

5. The infusion is complete when beads of moisture appear on the plant material. Preservation time varies from less than a week for plants with thin leaves, such as beech and small maples, to one month for those with thick leaves, such as laurel, fig, or ivy (see the list below for treatment periods for different plants). Remove the plants and pat off the moisture.

6. Store preserved materials in a cool, dry room until needed for wreaths, bouquets, or garlands.

Combine one part glycerine with two parts hot water.

To preserve berries, immerse them in the glycerine-and-water solution for two to three weeks.

If during this preservation process the tips of some leaves dry out, it means that they are receiving moisture too slowly. Apply the solution directly to the leaves with cotton balls or submerge the plants completely in the solution. When the color changes or the leaves glisten and show no signs or sounds of brittleness, remove the materials from the solution and store.

The following list gives approximate soaking times for different plants:

Bay—2 to 3 weeks; leaves darken in solution.

Beech—1 week.

Blackberries—3 weeks for leaves and berries.

Holly—3 weeks for leaves and berries; spray berries afterward with hair spray to make them shine.

Ivy—2 to 3 weeks; leaves turn dark and change.

Maple—2 weeks; will not last unless preserved in glycerine.

Oak—2 to 3 weeks; leaves and acorns preserve well on stems; leaves keep their color.

Rose hips—2 to 3 weeks; spray with clear lacquer after preserving.

Rosemary—2 weeks; stems become silver gray; scent is retained in leaves that turn dark green.

Rowan or mountain ash—2 to 3 weeks; spray berries with clear lacquer after treatment.

Space, Supplies, and Tools

Having a nice work space and the right supplies and tools, makes the craft of wreath making easier and more enjoyable. You will need a large work table in a well-lighted, well-ventilated room. Wreath making tends to be messy, so select a location where you can keep your materials ready and not be concerned about the bits and pieces that scatter about as you work. Gather the following supplies and have them accessible when you are ready to create your wreaths.

A good work space for wreath making is one where you do not have to worry about bits and pieces scattering about.

WIRE FRAMES, also called crimped wire rings, are simply circles of wire made for wreaths bases. They are readily available and so inexpensive that we no longer have to make wreath frames from coat hangers or other wire. They come in many sizes: 14-inch, 12-inch, 10-inch frames, and even smaller. To the frame dimension you will add two or three inches of material, so that the finished size of a wreath on a 10-inch frame easily becomes 12 inches or as much as 14 inches.

Crimped wire rings are available in several sizes for use as wreath bases.

SPECIAL FRAMES for Advent wreaths include holders for candles. They are readily available in different sizes. Another special frame is the planting frame designed for living wreaths. These hold sphagnum moss and are placed on trays or plates for easy watering.

WIRE of various weights and types is an absolute necessity. You will need green-coated florist's wire for binding evergreens, and silver wire for artemisia and statice. Heavy wire is used for hanging large wreaths and for binding together materials of considerable weight. To save time while assembling wreaths, you might want to cut and bundle several pieces of wire ahead of time.

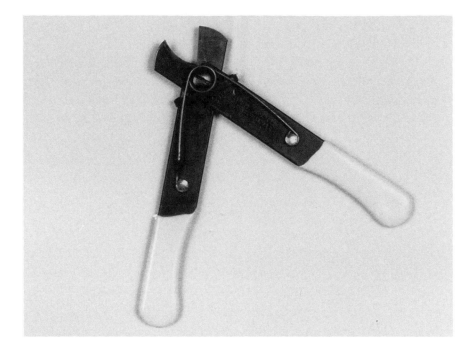

An electrician's tool makes a good combination flower and wire cutter.

A WIRE CUTTER AND STEM CUTTER may be combined in a single tool if you can find one that will cut all materials. The one we use at Caprilands was originally an electrician's tool and works efficiently as both a flower cutter and a wire cutter. It has a rounded tip so it can be carried in a pocket when not in use. It is steel and self-sharpening, and its use saves the garden shears. You may also need large garden clippers to cut heavy evergreens used in holiday decorations.

A GLUE GUN is a very handy device if you make a lot of wreaths. It is very helpful when you need to place small, unruly bits into a design.

AN ELECTRIC DRILL is necessary if you are using a lot of cinnamon sticks, gingerroots, nutmegs, tonka beans, and the like. These materials must be drilled and wired before you attach them to the wreath.

FINISHING SUPPLIES include sharp shears to cut ribbon or fabric and plastic spray to add sheen to leaves and berries. We prefer not to use sprays, though, because they tend to destroy the natural fragrances of herbs.

Once you've gathered your herbs, prepared your space, and assembled your tools and supplies, you are ready to begin wiring, snipping, and arranging herbs and flowers into whatever wreath design you imagine. At Caprilands, we make two basic kinds of wreaths, dried wreaths with artemisia bases and living wreaths.

Making Dried Wreaths

We make most of our dried wreaths with bases of the beautiful silver king artemisia and decorate them with dried herbs and flowers from the Caprilands gardens. On the following pages, you'll find the steps we take in assembling a dried wreath.

Making Artemisia Bases

To construct an artemisia base, we use stems of silver king with the curling tops removed. In addition to an ample supply of stems, you will need a wire wreath frame and a spool of lightweight wire to bind the artemisia to the frame.

Remove the curling tips from the artemisia stems before you begin constructing a wreath base.

Begin by bending the stems evenly around the wire frame, securing them together with wire as you go. Do not wire them too tightly. You will need room to insert sprigs of the silver tips into the base. Fragrant herbs such as tarragon, thyme, or sweet grass may also go into the base. If you don't have enough artemisia to make a full base, supplement it with straw or hay. Straw has a tendency to shed or to drop, so you will need to bind it more tightly than the artemisia. Cover the back of the base with strands of artemisia to give it a finished look; the front will be covered as you decorate it with textured and colorful herbs. Don't be afraid to beat the base into shape, for it must be an even circle. At Caprilands we say, "A wreath is only as good as its base." Many trimmings may come and go but a good base lasts indefinitely.

If your artemisia has been dried in baskets and has developed a nice curve, making the base will be easy. If your artemisia has been dried in a very hot place and is extremely stiff and difficult to use, try leaving it outside overnight to absorb moisture; or hold it over a steaming tea kettle or vaporizer to make it more pliable. No matter how careful you are or how pliable the artemisia is, bits and pieces will break and drop while you are making the base. (If you have to work in your kitchen or living room, spread a sheet under your work area to aid in cleanup). Don't discard these sprigs; on snowy days in the long winter all these precious pieces take on new value and may inspire you to make little nosegays called tussie mussies.

Arrange the stems evenly around the wire frame, bending them to conform to the circle.

Secure stems with wire, but leave room to insert sprigs of artemisia tips.

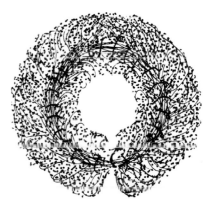

Make a good even circle.

Follow the same procedues for any wreath—large or small.

Tipping

When you are satisfied with your base, begin to cover it by inserting the feathery tips of the artemisia branches. We call this process "tipping." You may use individual sprays or prepared bundles. Turn the curls toward the center, working clockwise until the circle is filled. Shape the outside line carefully as you work in order to maintain a good circle. Control stragglers by wrapping wire lightly around the whole wreath and then covering the wire with more artemisia sprays. Save the laciest pieces for the center. Push them firmly into the framework, being careful to maintain a circle. Remember, nothing makes a wreath look scragglier than tips of branches running in all directions.

When inserting artemisia tips into a wreath base, place them so they all lie in the same direction

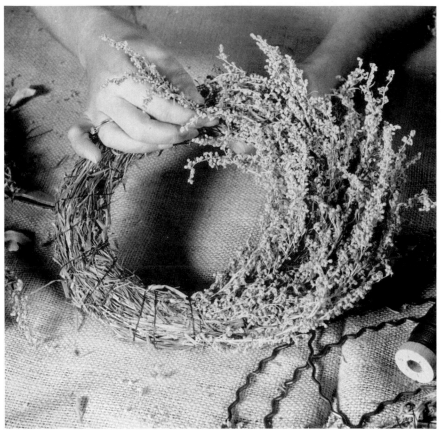

When adding artemisia tips, use the laciest pieces and turn the curling tips toward the center.

Push the tips firmly into the framework of the wreath base.

A view from the back.

Begin decorating after the base is complete. Leaves and flowers with stiff stems can be merely pushed in.

Decorating

After the base is completed, you are ready to add decorative material. Herbs and flowers should be picked, dried, or soaked in glycerine for the proper length of time. If you are making a flower wreath, flowers with weak stems, such as globe amaranth and strawflowers, should be wired before you add them. To wire a flower, you will need a 12-inch length of lightweight florist's wire. Gently but firmly push the end of the wire into the base of the bloom; hold the base of the bloom in one hand, and gradually twist the wire around the stem of the flower; then it is ready to insert into the wreath base.

If you are using spices, they need to be pierced and wired. Use a small bit to drill holes in nutmeg and cinnamon; then wire them together in bunches of three with lightweight florist's wire. Cardamom can be pierced with a sturdy needle or stiff wire.

Seedpods with stiff stems can be pushed into the wreath base without being reinforced with wire. Pinecones, though, are heavy and must be securely attached to the wreath by twisting an eight-inch piece of lightweight wire around the stem end of the cone and into the base. Sometimes very small cones can be wired together in bunches. You can also attach pinecones with a glue gun.

To add little bags of spices or potpourri, twist them closed with fine wire and attach them under the bow of the wreath. Often we wire them into the wreath base and tie a bow over them.

For a finishing touch, we usually place a bow at the bottom of the wreath.

Descriptions of many Caprilands wreaths are given in Part II of this book. Look through them for inspiration as you consider how you want to decorate your wreath.

Leaves may be wired together in bunches before adding them to a wreath.

Spices such as cinnamon, left, and nutmeg, right, and flowers with weak stems, center, must be wired before you add them to a wreath.

Making a Victorian Wreath

As an example of wreath construction, the following takes you step by step through the process of making a Victorian wreath.

To make the base, you will need a crimped wire wreath frame, a spool of lightweight wire, and plenty of the whitest and best silver king artemisia with curling tips that look like silver lace. For decora-

Combine various delicate flowers on a base of your best silver king artemisia for a lovely Victorian wreath.

tion gather together yellow strawflowers, pearly or sweet everlastings, small yarrows, pink globe amaranth, bits of blue salvia, lavender, and dried rosebuds wired together into sweet-smelling bunches of three. Be sure the color scheme includes varying shades of pink, yellow, white, light blue, and mauve. To complete the wreath, you will need a satin or velvet bow in the color of your choice. If you wish, tie a piece of lace into the bow for accent.

1. Begin your wreath by constructing the base of silver king artemisia. First remove the curling tops that are the decorative part of the plant. Arrange the stems around the wire frame, overlapping them in order to cover the frame thickly and evenly. Press them down and bind them lightly into place with lightweight florist's wire, leaving 1 to 2 inches between the strands as you wrap it around the wreath. Flatten the artemisia with both hands, adding more wire if necessary. Do not wrap the artemisia too tightly because you will insert the silver tips of the artemisia into the base. Be sure to keep an even circle as you work.

2. When the base is firm, begin to insert the curling feathery tips into it as described previously under "Tipping." This completes the base, and now it is ready to be decorated.

3. Many of the flowers used in a Victorian wreath will need to be wired before you can insert them into the design, especially the yellow strawflowers and pink globe amaranth (see instructions for wiring flowers earlier under "Decorating"). To add flowers to the wreath simply push the wired stems into the base, placing them about halfway between the inner and the outer edges of the wreath base and arranging them to please your eye. Gather together an odd number of rosebud clusters (probably five) and place them randomly around the circle, leaving a space at the bottom for the bow. Now fill in with pearly everlastings, small yarrows, and bits of blue salvia, pressing their soft stems among the sturdier ones already in the wreath. When the flowers are all placed, gently reshape the artemisia by adding small curved pieces where needed.

4. When your design is complete, make a bow of velvet or satin ribbon in a color that complements the color scheme of the wreath. Thread a wire through the back of the bow and use this wire to attach the bow to the base. To accent the bow you may want to tie in a piece of lace or a potpourri of sweet-smelling herbs such as lavender, sweet violets, or lilac. Now your wreath is ready to be enjoyed!

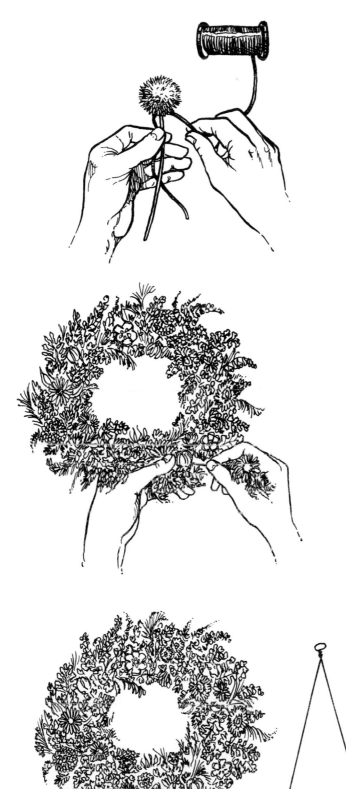

To wire a flower, cut off the stem. Then cut a piece of heavy wire to the desired length and push it into the base of the flower head. Take fine wire and wrap it around the wire stem, getting as close to the base of the flower as possible. Knot the fine wire before you cut it off.

Insert a wired flower the same way you do a flower with a stiff stem—just push it firmly into the base.

To make a hanger for your wreath, twist a piece of wire to form a small loop in the center. Then work the ends of the wire into the framework of the wreath to secure them.

Making Living Wreaths

Planting frames, now sold commercially for living wreaths, were unknown years ago. We had to make our own. My first one was made with a coat hanger pulled into a rather misshapen circle and bound with sphagnum moss loosely held together with wire. We gathered the moss from our swamp. It was greener than the commercial product and rather pretty in itself. With patience and perseverance we succeeded in making a fair foundation.

Now we purchase planting frames in many sizes in craft stores and garden centers. If you go looking for them in craft stores, they may not be called planting frames because they are also used for making pinecone wreaths. Look for wreath forms made with four concentric circles of wire and cross-braced with wire so that they have some height or depth. Ten-inch frames or larger work best for living wreaths.

A living wreath is made on a wire frame readily available in craft stores. You will also need a tray of similar size to place under the wreath to hold the moisture.

Sphagnum moss grows wild in bogs and brooks, but you can purchase it at a garden center. It comes in five- or ten-pound packages.

To make the wreath base, pack the frame with moss and then soak the moss thoroughly with water. Then begin inserting the plants. Our original evergreen base was made with small cuttings of juniper and a circle of boxwood. We still use this base for our Advent wreaths.

Carefully remove the plants from their pots.

Insert the plants between the wires of the frame.

To decorate the base we nestled into the moss a circle of green santolina cuttings, carefully covering the stems to encourage rooting in the damp sphagnum. Lavender and rosemary cuttings may be inserted in patterns, with the hope that some will root and live through the winter. Ivies especially like this medium. Sweet woodruff does well, too. It thrives in the moisture and doesn't need much sun to grow; some even has blossomed for us. Small cuttings of sage are decorative, and if they root, the flowering tips may produce blue blossoms.

Living wreaths must be put on trays to hold moisture and to make watering possible. A round aluminum or stainless steel tray is the most practical, and the rim of the tray frames the wreath nicely. We placed one of our most extravagant creations on a large pewter plate; the dull glow of the pewter complemented the grays and greens of the wreath.

If kept moist, a living wreath lasts almost indefinitely. Water the moss at least once a week; if sun hits it, water it every three days. Do not let it dry out.

Use sphagnum moss to fill in the spaces between the plants and wrap the entire frame with wire to secure the plants.

If you wish, cover the center of the tray under the wreath with fresh green moss.

At Caprilands we use living wreaths around punch bowls.

At Caprilands we set large living wreaths around punch bowls. In the spring we push daffodil stems into the wreath; in summer, roses. As the season progresses we add dahlias, nasturiums, calendulas, marigolds, and holly and ivy for Christmas. Flowers keep for a long period in the moist moss.

Making Garlands

Garlands can be made from materials collected from flowering fields or from your garden. Start by braiding together wildflowers, such as daisies and buttercups, with ferns and grasses. Insert clusters of clovers and daisies into each strand; they will create a lovely background for other colorful flowers you may wish to add. When adding flowers to the garland, you can simply insert the stems into the braid or use florist's wire to hold them in place.

You might consider making the base of the garland from bay, juniper, or a combination of both. Sweet Annie, pearly everlastings, silver leaves of artemisias, or roses finish the decoration. We have made very long garlands, using all of these plants, and draped them over the bride's chair for a wedding luncheon. We also hang them over doors through which the bride passes.

To make a casual flower rope of grasses or wildflowers...

Bind a few stems of flowers or grasses together with fine wire. Knot the wire firmly around the stems, take several turns around the length of the stems, and finish with a knot, but do not cut the wire.

Position a second bunch of flowers over the stems of the first and continue, first tying a knot, then wrapping the stems, this time joining the stems of both bunches. Secure with a knot before adding a third bunch. Proceed until flower rope is of desired length.

You may wish to tie the bunches of stems around a rope or wire for added security or firmness. If you do so, be sure to leave enough length at each end to make loops for hanging.

Kitchen Garlands

For a kitchen garland, we cut bunches of thyme, tarragon, rosemary, marjoram, sage, and basil, and wire these to a frame. They dry nicely and can be picked from the garland when needed to season recipes. Sometimes we wire together bay leaves and insert them into the garland as well.

Braided mints make an attractive and fragrant kitchen garland also. Use tall stems. Apple mint works best because the stems are strong. To this we add peppermint and a generous amount of orange mint.

To make a formal garland or rope of short-stemmed flowers or herbs...

Hold a bunch of stems firmly against some wire, and bind them securely with fine wire, beginning and finishing off with a knot. Without cutting the wire, place a second bunch, and proceed to knot and wrap with the wire until flower rope is of desired length.

A garland of short-stemmed flowers or herbs must be tied around a wire or rope. Leave enough length at each end for a loop or to attach by tying.

The garden at Caprilands abounds with a variety of textures, colors, and fragrances. We mix and match our plants to make all kinds of garlands.

A formal garland of short-stemmed flowers and herbs decorates the top of a white iron gate for a festive occasion outdoors.

A formal bouquet (on a round florist's foam base) tops the gatepost and completes the formal garland.

To make a firm base for a heavy garland or for weak-stemmed foliage...

Make a base of straw, artemisia, dill or other stems. Tie or bind the material securely around a rope or wire with cording, raffia, or wire. Stems may be inserted into this base as with a wreath. If the base is attractive, you don't need to cover it completely. Herbs, flowers, and spices may be inserted or wired in singly or in bunches.

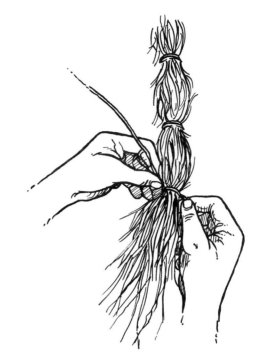

A swag or festoon of autumn grasses makes an attractive accent for a rope or garland.

Decorate a heavy garland base as you would a wreath.

Autumn Garlands

For autumn decor, we make a golden garland from a base of braided stems of sweet Annie. To this we add tansy, goldenrod, and small sunflowers. Strawflowers may also be used to dress this garland, but they must be wired first. The possibilities for an autumn garland seem endless. You can choose from zinnias, hardy chrysanthemums, small dahlia blossoms, and marigolds. These flowers will keep for a day or two; then replace them with early red rose hips, mountain ash berries, or brilliant black alder.

Other possible plants for fall garlands include wild clematis (*Clematis vitalba*), bittersweet (*Solanum dulcamara*), and highbush cranberry (*Viburnum trilobum*). You can find wild clematis on neglected roadsides. Its blossoms turn into a white fluff that clings to the vine. Placed around grapevines, it makes a wonderful "witchy" garland that can be draped across a window or fireplace mantle with a witch's broom added for accent.

Bittersweet is very decorative in the fall. We hang it from our beamed ceilings in various buildings during September and October. For autumn, nothing quite compares to a garland twined from grapevines and bittersweet with its scarlet berries. Bittersweet alone adds a bright touch to a mantle.

Another beautiful plant is the highbush cranberry. Its white blossoms of spring turn into heavy clusters of deep red berries by fall. These berries remain on the branches through the winter. Some people use them to make jellies, jams, or pies, but the odor of the crushed berry is repulsive. We use them in autumn decorations placed high and away from exploring fingers.

Use your imagination to combine wreaths, swags, dried flowers and foliage, like those on these pages, with other decorative elements to give your home and workplace a charming warmth in the fall.

Christmas House Garlands

A permanent frieze of pinecones surrounds the 18th century Caprilands kitchen room, which now serves as our main dining room. We made this frieze with various sizes and kinds of cones, most native to New England, wired together to form a patterned garland. The pinecones remain in place year round.

For our Christmas decorations, which go up in November, we make excursions into the woods to gather loads of creeping club moss (*Lycopodium obscurum*). Each year we take this from a different area and are careful cutting it so that the roots remain in the ground to renew for another year. After we harvest the moss, we bind it into strands of four. We cut off all the brown parts and then force the bound strands behind the pinecones that form the permanent garlands in our dining room. We work quickly to bind and place the moss, because when hung to dry indoors overnight, it stays bright green until spring.

After the Christmas season, which lasts until February 2 at Caprilands, we hang boxwood. It lessens the dull feeling we invariably have when all our lavish Christmas decorations are removed, and it carries us until we ready the walls and ceilings for spring.

To wire a pinecone for attaching to a wreath, garland, or frieze...

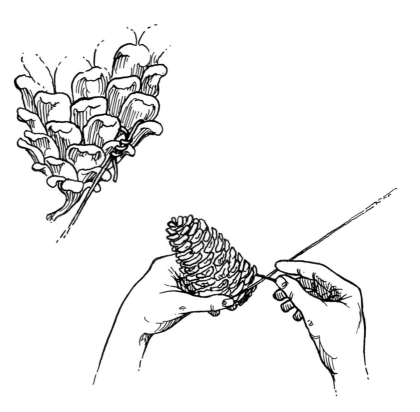

Loop a medium-weight wire around one of the lowest bands of scales. Twist several tight turns in the wire as close to the base of the cone as possible. Be sure to leave a long enough length of wire to attach the cone to the wreath or garland.

Caprilands Wreath Party

To dramatize and celebrate the labor of wreath making, Caprilands planned and gave a party in honor of this ancient craft. We formed all the foods in a wreath shape or decorated them with a wreath pattern. You, too, might want to celebrate your efforts by throwing a party.

For a bright table centerpiece, we arranged colorful salads in the form of a wreath on a large plate. These were both delightful and delicious. We garnished the outer edge of the salad plate with tender, delicate orange and apple mint leaves. The contrast in colors and odors of the mints pleased us. Orange mint has the perfume of fruit and flowers, and the apple mint releases, of course, the scent of apples. Along with the mint leaves, we arranged slices of apples and pears lightly coated with salad dressing and sprinkled with finely chopped

A wreath party provides a great opportunity to share the pleasure of wreath making with friends.

toasted almonds and a dash of caraway or sesame seeds. Use your imagination to create wreath salads for your own wreath party.

Bread baked in the shape of wreaths accompanied the salads. Many recipes for attractive wreath breads can be found among traditional Christmas recipes. Our Caprilands green spinach bread makes a very handsome green wreath bread, which we decorate with leaves and raisins or currants. Any other wreath bread would be appropriate also.

If a garden is at hand, wreath makers may add some fresh leaves and flowers to the wreaths.

Making wreaths outside takes the messiness of the activity out of the house.

For dessert we served punch and cake and cookies decorated in wreath designs. Cakes can be made in the shape of wreaths, or you can decorate a sheet cake with geranium leaves arranged in the form of two wreaths, as we do. We place tiny dried rosebuds between the leaves for color and extra scent. Make wreath-shaped cookies with a doughnut cutter or cookie molds. Decorate them with raisins, nuts, and green mint leaves. And be sure to put a living wreath around the punch bowl as we always do at Caprilands.

Happy Wreath Making!

Plan your wreath party as a workshop. This means having plenty of materials on hand for everyone—wire frames, quantities of artemisia, spools of wire, cutting tools for artemisia and flowers, and the trimmings: dried flowers, bunches of spices such as cinnamon sticks and nutmegs, and ribbons.

Work on large tables in an area where the messiness of this activity will not be a problem. The kitchen, basement, garage, or porch will do. Place sheets under the work tables to collect debris for quick cleanup. And don't forget to save the scraps from your work. What a pleasant way to spend an afternoon, and everyone has something special to take home!

A spinning wheel makes a handy lap-top table when working on wreaths outdoors.

CATALOG OF HERBS AND FLOWERS

Artemisia
Artemisia spp.

So gentle is she, Artemis the Holy
To dewy youth, to tender nurselings
The young, of all that roam the meadow,
Of all who live within the forest.
—Edith Hamilton

Description

Many varieties of artemisia can be used in wreath making: mugwort (*A. vulgaris*), silver king (*A. ludoviciana albula*), southernwood (*A. abrotanum*), sweet Annie (*A. annua*), and wormwood (*A. absinthium*), to name a few. The plants provide profuse quantities of feathery plumes for long lasting, fragrant dried material. Most have silvery foliage, but some are brownish gray or even yellow-green.

Lore and Meaning
Dignity; protection from disease and misfortune.

Culture and Harvest
Artemisias are more easily grown from cuttings and root divisions than from seed. They self sow, so be sure to pull out seedlings growing where you do not want them. Harvest the foliage in the middle of September, but leave some until later. When mature, artemisias turn a lovely warm brown with creamy, almost white, seeds.

Preservation and Use
Hang bunches of stems in a dry, well-ventilated room. Artemisia makes a solid base for fragrant wreaths and provides an attractive background for small flowers. Long stems, when fresh and pliable, can be easily twisted into a crown, or you can tie or wire small bunches to a wreath frame. The tips of small branches add a lacy, delicate look to wreaths and other decorations.

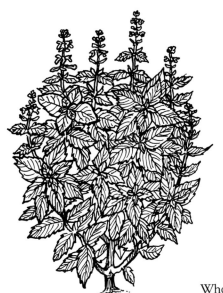

Basil
Ocimum basilicum

With Basil then I will begin
Whose scent is wondrous pleasing.
—Drayton

Description
Basil is a favorite kitchen herb that has a clovelike odor and flavor. Its bright green, toothed leaves are very fragrant, especially in the sun, but they wilt quickly. Its many varieties include small-leafed, bush, lemon, purple (also called dark opal), cinnamon, and several more.

Lore and Meaning
Honor to the dead, poverty, love; purifies the air, drives away infection. In Greek churches on special days, small sprigs of basil are used to sprinkle holy water at special ceremonies.

Culture and Harvest
Basil is an annual that grows easily from seed and likes the hottest weather. Sow seeds three times during the year for a constant fresh crop during the summer months. It likes a rich soil, although it grows well in average soil. To keep basil growing, harvest from the top to prevent plant from going to seed. The seeds come very quickly during the growing season, so cut the plant once each week.

Preservation and Use

Basil for wreaths must be used fresh from the garden since it wilts quickly. A kitchen wreath of basil is practical for use if supported with other herbs. Insert it with other stiff-leafed shrubby herbs such as thyme or sage to hold it in place, or tie it in bunches and attach it close to the wreath base. It adds a powerful fragrance. You can also make a kitchen wreath using basil leaves and wiring in cloves of garlic like nuts.

Bay
Laurus nobilis

Let wreaths of triumph now my temples twine
The victor cried, the glorious prize is mine
Accept, O Garth, the Muse's early lays
That adds this wreath of Ivy to thy bays.
—Anonymous

Description

In New England, *Laurus* grows as a tender perennial and seldom reaches more than six feet in height. In its native home along the Mediterranean, though, it may grow to 60 feet. Its beautiful dark green leaves are mildly fragrant and very flavorful.

Lore and Meaning

A mark of achievement, distinction, and superiority. It reputedly protects against the ravages of thunder and lightning. Its condition is indicative of success or disaster in the family or in the nation.

Culture and Harvest

Propagate bay from cuttings, which take about six months to root. Because it thrives in partial shade, it makes a great houseplant. It also grows well in tubs as a city tree since its thick leaves resist pollution.

Preservation and Use

Large old bays yield many fine leaves for wreath making. If treated with glycerine, the leaves remain deep green and pliable indefinitely; however, they are generally used fresh and allowed to dry in the wreath. Dry leaves can be wired to a wreath base if handled carefully; they do tend to break. To make a crown of bay, tie bay leaves in flat bunches and wire them together to form a continuous circle. Bay leaves are an important culinary herb in a kitchen wreath.

Borage
Borago officinalis

Here is sweet water and Borage for blending,
Comfort and courage to drink to your fill.
—Norah Hopper

Description
Borage is a leafy, many branched herb. Its large, grayish green, hairy leaves taste and smell like cucumbers. It produces striking bright blue flowers that are shaped like stars.

Lore and Meaning
Comfort, courage; said to drive away melancholy.

Culture and Harvest
Borage is a hardy annual. Seeds sown either in fall or spring will produce a good stand. Plant borage in full sun, sowing more than once a year for continued bloom. Borage often self sows; you may find little seedlings coming up in spring.

Preservation and Use
Surround a punch bowl with fresh flowers and leaves. Combine borage with a lemon balm, thyme, and salad burnet in an attractive and fragrant fresh wreath, or insert the leaves and flowers in the moist sphagnum of a living wreath.

Boxwood
Buxus sempervirens

Get ye all three into Box-tree.
—Shakespeare

Description
Boxwood is an evergreen shrub or tree with many small, dark green, lustrous leaves. It is well suited for shaping into topiary forms such as animals and the once popular mazes.

Lore and Meaning
Immortality; dedicated to the god, Pluto, who symbolized the continuation of life in the infernal regions.

Culture and Harvest
Boxwood grows well in ordinary, well-drained soil and thrives in shade or sun. It grows slowly from seed and is best propagated from hardwood cuttings. Set new plants in the ground in late summer or early spring.

Preservation and Use
Boxwood dries green and remains so indefinitely. At Caprilands we use fresh branches and insert them into the moist sphagnum of our living wreaths. Boxwood may be tied in bunches and wired to a wreath base or inserted into an artemisia base. It creates a good dark green background, which accentuates the color of field flowers and silver herbs. Garlands of boxwood make attractive house decorations. At Caprilands we make a very large wreath of boxwood at Midsummer, and decorate it with symbolic plants of the season, including vervain, daisies, mugwort, and ferns.

Broom
Cytisus scoparius

If you sweep the house with broom in May,
You'll sweep the head of the house away.
—Dutch proverb

Description
Broom is a deciduous shrub, which grows wild in the British Isles and on the European continent. It lines highways in Greece and Sicily. Its long slender branches are almost leafless, and it produces yellow pea-shaped flowers.

Lore and Meaning
There is an old Dutch saying that if you hang out the broom, you are looking for a second husband.

Culture and Harvest
Broom prefers poor soil with good drainage in a site fully exposed to the sun. It even tolerates a lot of wind. Broom grows readily from seed, and also can be propagated from cuttings.

Preservation and Use
Broom branches should be shaped while still pliable. Quite decorative, they make excellent witch's brooms and quick and easy wreaths.

Chamomile
Chamaemelum nobile

Though the chamomile, the more it is trodden on, the faster it grows, yet youth, the more it is wasted, the sooner it wears.
—Shakespeare

Description
Chamomile flowers look like small daisies. The foliage of this plant is fine and fernlike. Chamomile abounds in spring. The flowers you pick in autumn are the plant's second growth.

Lore and Meaning
Humility, sweetness; used to calm the body and mind and to help overcome weariness. A famous old-world plant, it is both friendly and beneficial.

Culture and Harvest
Chamomile will grow in sun and partial shade in moist, well-drained soil. Sow seeds in spring or fall. Once established, it will self sow.

Preservation and Use
Chamomile can be used fresh or dried. Tie chamomile in compact bunches of about four stems and force these into the green background of a living wreath or a fresh herb wreath. They are attractive combined with mint, sage, thyme, and rosemary. The dried flower heads may be brewed for tea, so they are appropriate for tea wreaths.

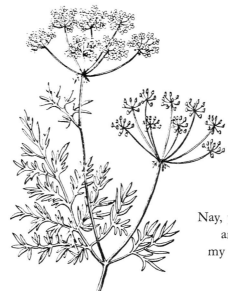

Caraway
Carum carvi

Nay, you shall see my orchard, where, in an arbour we will eat a last year's pippin of my own grafting, with a dish of caraways.
—Shakespeare

Description
Caraway is a hardy biennial and grows to a height of one to three feet. Its stems are furrowed, and its finely cut leaves resemble those of a carrot. Umbels of white flowers bloom in June of the second year.

Lore and Meaning
Prevents theft, strengthens vision; brings straying husbands home.

Culture and Harvest
Caraway grows best in full sun in an average, well-drained soil. Sow seeds in September for an early spring crop of leaves and seeds. If you wish to use the umbels for decoration, pick them as soon as they are completely open.

Preservation and Use
Caraway has many culinary uses in seed cakes, breads, and cookies and so is an appropriate herb for kitchen wreaths. Fresh caraway greens make a very fragrant wreath base when used alone or bound with other cooking herbs such as thyme, rosemary, and marjoram. The seed heads can be used fresh or dried to decorate wreaths.

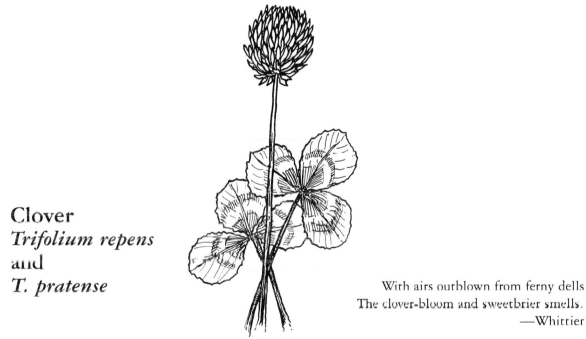

Clover
Trifolium repens
and
T. pratense

With airs outblown from ferny dells
The clover-bloom and sweetbrier smells.
—Whittier

Description
Clover has dense pink or white globe-shaped flower heads with a faint sweet scent. The leaves have three leaflets and are quite tender.

Lore and Meaning
Symbolizes the Trinity; supposedly aids in the detection of witches.

Culture and Harvest
Both varieties of clover grow wild in fields and meadows. Harvest them throughout the growing season.

Preservation and Use
Soft and pliant wreaths and garlands can be braided from clover, but they are not firm enough to hang well. In former times, farmers placed such wreaths around the necks of animals for the midsummer celebration. Made from edible flowers and without harmful wire, they were safe for the animals to wear. We still make wreaths for animals from a braided clover base. For a firmer base and a more permanent decoration, we add artemisia.

Daisy
Chrysanthemum leucanthemum

Young men and maids meet
To exercise their dancing feet
Tripping the comely country round
With Daffodils and Daisies crowned.
—Herrick

Description
The oxeye daisy, the familiar wild white daisy of the eastern United States is a European native, which has been long naturalized in our fields and pastures. Few things recall youth and innocence more than the daisy.

Lore and Meaning
Purity in thought; loyal love.

Culture and Harvest
The wild daisy is a common weed. The true English daisy (*Bellis perennis*) can be grown from seed but must have winter protection. These cultivated daisies do not survive scorching hot July days but make beautiful border plants in the spring.

Preservation and Use
Daisies are generally used green, not dried. They last several days if picked fresh and inserted into a wet sphagnum moss base. They may be dried in silica gel; however the results are hardly worth the expense and trouble. Daisies are set off nicely in a fresh wreath with a fern base. Also, their strong stems can be braided easily into a fresh daisy wreath.

Dill
Anethum graveolens

There with her Valerian and her Dill
That hindereth witches of their will.
—Michael Drayton

Description
Dill is a culinary herb with flavorsome, lacy green leaves, decorative seed heads, and very strong stems. It lasts a long time in water.

Lore and Meaning
Quiets or lulls; gives protection from witches.

Culture and Harvest
Dill grows well from seed. It self sows, and is treated as an annual. Make two plantings, one in early spring, the other about July 1, to have fresh dill in the garden all season long. Grow it in rich composted soil for best results.

Preservation and Use
Dill may be hung in bunches to dry. For best results, though, poke holes through a box top and thread the stems through the holes so the seed head rests on the lid. Place the top back on the box and leave the plants to dry. Use the umbels in witch's wreaths, kitchen wreaths, and in table decorations.

Elder
Sambucus canadensis

Bourtree, Bourtree, crooked rong
Never straight and never strong
Ever bush and never tree
Since our Lord was nailed to thee.
—Anonymous

Description
The North American variety of elder is a stalky shrub that produces clusters of small white flowers. Its purplish black berries are often used to make jelly. The European, or black elder (*S. nigra*), grows to 30 feet and bears yellowish white flowers and black, shiny berries. The elder played a prominent part in folklore and was called the boor tree.

Lore and Meaning
Protection against witches.

Culture and Harvest
This hardy shrub thrives in rich, moist soil under some shade. Propagate it by cuttings or seed. Pick blossoms in June and July and berry-laden branches later.

Preservation and Use
Elderberries look best in wild wreaths. We add the woody branches to witch's wreaths because they represented magic, not because they are very decorative. Spray the berries with plastic to prevent them from drying. This is not a permanent decoration.

Fennel
Foeniculum vulgare

Above the lower plants it towers,
The Fennel with its yellow flowers;
And in an earlier age than ours
Was gifted with the wondrous powers
Lost vision to restore.
—Longfellow

Description
Fennel adds wonderful flavor to foods. It grows tall and looks somewhat like dill with its delicate umbels of yellow flowers, which later turn to seed. The celerylike stems taste like anise and are very good in salads.

Lore and Meaning
Restores vision; gives strength in combat.

Culture and Harvest
Grow fennel from seed in enriched garden soil. Cut the flower heads for decoration as soon as they form an attractive umbel.

Preservation and Use
The umbels may be used green or dried. When drying them follow the same procedure as used for dill. Fennel foliage can be formed or braided into a fragrant base for a kitchen wreath.

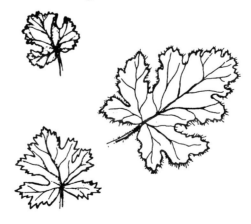

Geranium, Scented
Pelargonium, spp.

The fragrant geranium has nostalgic charm in every leaf. Touching the lacy cut leaves of the rose is like rubbing a magic jar from which a fragrant smoke quickly rises and coils around a rococo picture of the past.
—Adelma Simmons

Description

The scented geraniums are only distantly related to the rest of the geraniums. The genus, *Pelargonium*, is the Latin name for stork, and was given to these plants because the seed case of the blossom resembles a stork's bill. The leaves vary in shape, and their textures range from velvety to sticky. The scents of the many varieties are as distinct as the fruits or flowers for which they are named: apple, pineapple, rose, mint, and nutmeg, to name a few.

Lore and Meaning

The different scents have different meanings: rose, I prefer you; nutmeg, an expected meeting.

Culture and Harvest

Scented geraniums are tender and thrive in cool, sunny windows in the winter. Plant them outside as soon as the danger of frost has past. They prefer a dry, well-drained rich soil and a sunny location. Bring them in or take cuttings early in the fall.

Preservation and Use

Use scented geraniums in living wreaths. To preserve the leaves, dry them quickly away from light or press them between sheets of absorbent paper or on a blotter under a sheet of glass. Dried this way, they will retain their green color. The leaves are very fragrant and are more useful than the tiny flowers.

Goutweed
Aegopodium podagraria

The very bearing of it about one eases the pains of gout and defends him that bears it from the disease.
—Gerard

Description

Goutweed is a prolific plant. It makes a handsome and permanent border in a variegated garden. The leaves are white and green and sharply marked; the stem brown with a purple tinge. Both leaves and stems are sturdy.

Lore and Meaning

Eases pain and protects.

Culture and Harvest

Goutweed is easily grown, too easily many gardeners feel. A hardy perennial, it spreads rapidly in either sun or shade. It is often planted as a ground cover.

Preservation and Use

Used fresh, the sturdy leaves and stems can be twisted into a wreath base, garland, or crown. Decorate these with white flowers, baby's breath, sweet everlastings, daisies, and the like. They will last for several days. You also might weave the leaves into braided clover stems to make a base.

Holly
Ilex verticillata

Holly he hath berries as red as any rose,
The foresters, the hunters keep them from the does;
—Old Song

Description

Wild Holly is also called winterberry. It is a shrub or sometimes small tree with prickly, shiny leaves and bright berries. In November and early December, the berries are a blaze of color.

Lore and Meaning

Protection from witchcraft.

Culture and Harvest

Holly grows best in the moist air and sandy, slightly acid soils along the Eastern seaboard. Many cultivated varieties exist and some species grow in the wild. Only the female trees bear fruit but need a male tree nearby for pollination. If you don't grow holly or know of any wild shrubs, you can purchase branches of it during the Christmas season.

Preservation and Use

Holly looks best when used fresh in a living wreath. If used in a dry wreath or arrangement, spray it with plastic spray to keep the leaves in shape. Soaking branches in a glycerine solution will preserve them permanently.

Ivy
Hedera spp.

The rich evergreen of the Ivy never sears. Milton recommended it to the Romans to be joined with the Bay in the Chaplets of poets.
—Shakespeare

Description
Ivy, a wild vining plant in Europe, Asia, and Africa, has many beautiful varieties. Some have white and pink coloring in the leaves, and others gold. The leaves vary greatly in size and lobe pattern.

Lore and Meaning
Knowledge.

Culture and Harvest
Cuttings from this hardy vine root easily. Some of the fancier, delicate varieties should be moved inside for the winter. They require very little sun to survive.

Preservation and Use
Use ivy in living wreaths, or twist or braid the long strong stems into a crown. In ancient times it was entwined with grapes and donned the heads of those who led the good life of wine and song.

Juniper
Juniperus sabina

And with grass stills, and sticks of Juniper
Raise the black spright that burns not with the fire.
—Halls Satires

Description
Juniper is one of the most valued evergreens for Christmas decorations. The spreading branches are covered with silver-blue berries.

Lore and Meaning
Drives away witches, protects.

Culture and Harvest
Juniper grows wild in pastures and woodlands. Many cultivated varieties are used in landscaping. It prefers a light loamy soil and full sun. Both male and female shrubs must be grown for the female plant to produce berries.

Preservation and Use
Use juniper fresh, but keep in it water until you need it. Insert branches in the moist sphagnum moss of living wreaths and decorate with red berries or flowers.

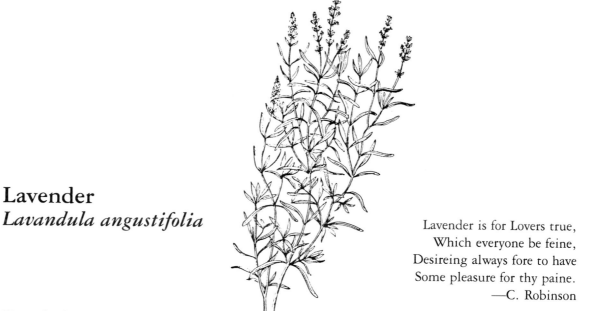

Lavender
Lavandula angustifolia

Lavender is for Lovers true,
Which everyone be feine,
Desireing always fore to have
Some pleasure for thy paine.
—C. Robinson

Description
Nearly everyone knows the strong sweet fragrance of lavender. This perennial herb is characterized by needlelike gray-green leaves and spikes of lavender flowers.

Lore and Meaning
Undying love, purity, sweetness, cleanliness.

Culture and Harvest
Lavender seed does not always germinate and when it does, it grows slowly. So take slips of lavender with the heel (the curved base of the shoot) attached and root them in moist sand. Do this in July. Divisions may be made after the plant blooms. Lavender can be harvested in late June, July, and sometimes August. Once the blossoms are cut, it may bloom a second time. When harvesting, cut the blossom stem down to where it joins the main body of the plant. Blossoms open slowly and often show some color weeks before they expand.

Preservation and Use
Put cut stems in containers without water, or use only a little water and let it dry out. If the flowers are not fully opened, leave the stems until the water evaporates. We use lavender in Victorian and wedding wreaths and wherever fragrance and blue color are needed. Make small wreaths of lavender for gifts or to encircle candlesticks.

Lemon Balm
Melissa officinalis

Melissophyllon, Balm hath an admirable
virtue to alter melancholy,
be it steeped in our ordinary drink,
extracted or otherwise taken.
—Burton

Description

Lemon balm is a fragrant green herb with a lemon scent that lasts for days. Its leaves are heart shaped. The flowers are bluish-white or yellow and occur in loose bunches in the axils of the leaves.

Lore and Meaning

Ensures long life; combats melancholy.

Culture and Harvest

This fairly hardy perennial may be grown from seed, planted in either spring or fall; it self sows in some situations. Pick when you are ready to use it.

Preservation and Use

Lemon balm leaves do not dry well but will last several days in a fresh wreath. Field flowers such as yellow or white daisies may be woven into it for decoration. Add a yellow bow with streamers for a sunny look.

Lemon Verbena
Aloysia triphylla

It grows along the old cathedral wall,
Where volcano shadows fall,
Herba Luisa of sweetest smell
Makes a tea as well.
—Adelma Simmons

Description

A native of the Americas, lemon verbena is a tender plant that needs lots of attention in northern United States. It is a deciduous shrub with light green, lance-shaped leaves that have a delightful sweet, lemony fragrance. It often loses its leaves when moved inside in the fall. This plant is called *herba luisa* in Latin America.

Lore and Meaning

Healing.

Culture and Harvest

Lemon verbena can be trained as a topiary tree but is very sensitive to change. There is no readily available or viable seed; most plants are grown from cuttings and are not easily propagated.

Preservation and Use

Entire wreaths can be made of verbena. The very woody branches can be forced into the base thickly. Decorate with yellow strawflowers or white amaranth. Lemon verbena should be used in wreaths while fresh and allowed to dry on the wreath frame. Kept out of the sun, the leaves will stay green and continue to give off a very sweet odor. Circle a teapot with a small lemon verbena wreath as it is an important tea ingredient.

Lettuce
Lactuca sativa
(and other
garden varieties)

> Thou truly, to all tyrants are of use.
> Their madness flies before thy powerful juice
> Their heads with lettuce wreaths, I prithee crown,
> And let the world in them thy kindness own.
> —Cowley

Description
Lettuce grew in the wild in many parts of Europe. Its green leaves were so pleasing that it was soon cultivated in gardens. It was called sleepwort by the Anglo-Saxons. The more decorative garden varieties may be used for fresh wreaths.

Lore and Meaning
Sleep inducing, soothing.

Culture and Harvest
Sow seeds early in the spring because lettuce tends to go to seed in hot weather. For decorative purposes, harvest the most attractive leaves and keep them cool and moist until use.

Preservation and Use
Fresh lettuce, parsley, and dill entwined with thyme make an interesting small wreath to decorate a kitchen table. The leaves should be put into wet sphagnum moss in a planting frame. Placed on a plate and kept well watered, it should last several days. You can use several varieties of lettuce to make a wreath-shaped salad. Combine bronze, or oak leaf lettuce, with the more common types for lovely color. Decorate with olives and radishes.

Lilac
Syringa vulgaris

> I'll weave my love a Garland,
> It shall be dressed so fine,
> I'll set it round with roses
> With Lilacs, Pinks and Thyme.
> —The Loyal Lover

Description
This woody European shrub often grows wild in North America. Its leaves are heart shaped and green. The fragrant blossoms appear in showy panicles and may be white, blue, lavender, or almost red in color.

Lore and Meaning
Love (purple); purity, modesty, and innocence (white).

Culture and Harvest
Lilacs need sun and moisture to bloom. Purchase roots to cultivate them in your garden.

Preservation and Use
Use fresh blossoms and leaves in circles around punch bowls in spring. Dried seed heads can be used in autumn arrangements. Lilacs will not last long out of water, so insert stems in wet sphagnum moss. Small buds or segments of the lilac flower head blend nicely with pinks in a living wreath made on a base of thyme.

Linden
Tilia americana

Tales of old sorrow
Grieve us no more,
With Linden boughs
At Beauty's altar
Pay ye your vows.
—Medieval lyrics

Description
American lindens, also called basswoods, can grow to 130 feet. They have a nice shape, and you often see them lining driveways or city streets. Lindens produce sweet-smelling white to yellow flowers in spring, which attract bees.

Lore and Meaning
Flowering branches prevent intoxication when worn.

Culture and Harvest
Lindens can be grown from seed, cuttings, or grafting. They do well in most soils, but won't tolerate drought. Cut flowering branches to use in wreaths.

Preservation and Use
The flowering boughs add fragrance and variety to ordinary wreaths and garlands. In ancient times, floral chaplets worn by guests at feasts were tied with the bark of linden to prevent intoxication.

Love-Lies-Bleeding
Amaranthus caudatus

Silence and sleep
Like fields of Amaranth lie.
—Cowley

Description
This large herb, reaching three to five feet in height produces large bright red, nodding flower heads. The young leaves and the seeds of this plant are edible.

Lore and Meaning
Constancy, fidelity, immortality.

Culture and Harvest
These plants grow readily from seed and prefer full sun. They do best in average soils and in fact produce less brilliant blooms in fertile soils. Begin harvesting flowers when about half of them have opened.

Preservation and Use
Strip the leaves from the stems, and hang the flowers to dry. They add good color and texture to dried wreaths.

Marjoram
Origanum majorana

Indeed, sir, she was the sweet
Marjoram of the Salad, or rather
the Herb-of-grace.
—Shakespeare

Description
A popular herb among gardeners, marjoram is a tender perennial. It has fuzzy oval gray-green leaves, and in midsummer, white or pink flowers appear at the tips of the stems. Marjoram grows to a height of about one foot.

Lore and Meaning
Happiness, blushes.

Culture and Harvest
Marjoram is a tender perennial that is usually grown as an annual. It grows easily from seed and reaches a good size in one season. It must be harvested before the first frost.

Preservation and Use
Little bunches of fresh marjoram can be tied into a kitchen wreath, not only for fragrance, but also for use in seasoning. It can take the place of thyme in a wreath. For Christmas, thread a piece of ribbon through a firm apple. Insert stems of rosemary, marjoram, and oregano into the apple and dangle it from a wreath of marjoram.

Myrtle
Myrtus communis

> Venus with young Adonis sitting
> By her under a Myrtle shade
> Began to woo him.
> —Shakespeare

Description
A tender shrub with small decorative leaves and tiny white blossoms, the myrtle is very fragrant. In a warm climate the foliage has a very spicy accent.

Lore and Meaning
Virginity; the plant of love; thought by the Greeks to dispel the effect of wine.

Culture and Harvest
Myrtle is a tender plant. It can be grown outside in the South, but grow it in pots in the North so it can be brought indoors for the winter. It can be propagated by cuttings or seeds.

Preservation and Use
Myrtle has always been used in brides' crowns. In fact, it was customary in Sweden to give a young girl a myrtle plant to care for until her wedding day, when the leaves would be used for her crown. Fresh myrtle sprigs can be twined easily around a wire base or woven together to form a soft crown. Decorate the crown with white roses and white ribbons.

Oak
Quercus spp.

I adorned the Father of Midsummer Night
With a crown of oak leaves,
Thus may his sons grow
As robust as the mighty oak.
—Latvian poem

Description
The oak is a large common American shade tree with lobed leaves.

Lore and Meaning
Protection.

Culture and Harvest
Oaks can be propagated from seeds sown in autumn. They like rich, moist soil. Gather leaves in autumn for their color.

Preservation and Use
Leaves picked up from the ground may be used in wreaths untreated; however, to preserve colorful leaves for long-lasting use in wreaths, treat them with glycerine. Insert the leaf stems into a base of artemisia or matted ferns. Acorns can be drilled, wired, and added for decoration along with pinecones, dried fern fronds, and dark brown grasses.

Parsley
Petroselinum crispum

At Sparta's palace twenty beauteous maids
The pride of Greece, fresh garlands crowned their heads
with hyacinths and twining parsley drest,
Graced joyful Menelaus' marriage feast.
—Theocritus

Description
Parsley is a small, bright green, garden herb with feathery leaves that lie flat like celery, in the case of flat leaf parsley, or curl tightly as in the curly leaf variety. Chewing parsley freshens the breath.

Lore and Meaning
Honor, festivity; sometimes associated with death.

Culture and Harvest
Sow seeds in the garden in spring, or set out plants. Parsley is very hardy and, if mulched, will produce well into December.

Preservation and Use
Fresh parsley may be tied easily in bunches and added to a kitchen wreath. You might tie bunches of four to six stems of parsley to a base of artemisia covered with tarragon, or thick bunches may be tied onto a wire ring along with other herbs. Parsley can be placed in a living wreath in combination with other herbs. Use moist sphagnum moss for the base, and the plants will root in it.

Pinks
Dianthus spp.

Carnations and streaked gilly flowers,
the fairest flowers of the season.
—Perdita

Description
The *Dianthus* family includes many familiar flowers—carnations, sweet William, dianthus, and gilliflowers—as well as pinks. Pinks were once known as "sops of wine." They have a spicy smell and come in all shades of pink and red and in white. The stiff stems and foliage are gray-green in color. Carnations are also used in wreath making. The name "carnation" comes from "coronet."

Lore and Meaning
Disdain, woman's love, fascination.

Culture and Harvest
Pinks are easily grown from seed. Plant them in full sun in average, well-drained soil. They grow as annuals in zones 4 and lower.

Preservation and Use
Pinks and carnations dry well in silica gel, borax, or sand. Keep dried blooms out of the sun, for they fade easily. Fresh flowers add charm to bouquets, garlands, or crowns.

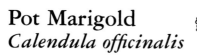

Pot Marigold
Calendula officinalis

Open afresh your round of starry folds
Ye ardent Marigolds.
—John Keats

Description
The pot marigold was the "golds" of Shakespeare's time. The flowers, of varying shades of yellow and orange, open at dawn and close in the evening. This type of marigold is not related to the common marigolds planted in flower gardens. Those are of the genus *Tagetes*.

Lore and Meaning
Joy; looking at it raises gloomy spirits.

Culture and Harvest
Grow pot marigolds from seed, but be certain your seed is fresh because it will not germinate after about a year. Marigolds bloom more quickly in rich soil. They will survive light frost. When harvesting, pick them at noon when they are fully open.

Preservation and Use
Insert fresh flowers into a wreath that has already been prepared. The stems are not very strong, so they may need to be wired first. Pot marigolds dry to a nice gold color, usually a shade deeper than when they were fresh. Handle them carefully; they are very fragile when dry.

Privet
Ligustrum vulgare

I tried to make a garland for the saints
All that this blockhead zeal of mine could find
Was privit blossom, falling as I touched it.
—Latin lyrics

Description

Privet is an evergreen shrub of the olive family. It produces small white flowers and blue-black berries. Its leaves are oblong to lance shaped and are about two inches long.

Lore and Meaning

Love.

Culture and Harvest

Privet makes an excellent green hedge in warm climates. They grow in average soil and can be propagated by cuttings, division, seeds, or grafting. For use in wreaths, harvest branches while flowers are young, so they won't drop off.

Preservation and Use

Fresh privet branches can easily be twisted into an attractive wreath and are a good substitute for boxwood. If you take branches while the flowers are young, the wreath will be especially attractive.

Rose
Rosa spp.

My mother raised me
In a garden of white roses
With a wreath of white roses
I myself adorned.
—Latvian folk song

Description

The rose, wild or cultivated, is a thorny-stemmed flowering shrub with showy blossoms in white, yellow, pink, and red, many of which are very fragrant. Roses have always held special meaning for brides and spring festivities.

Lore and Meaning

Beauty, youth, love; charm and innocence (white); love and desire (red).

Culture and Harvest

Plant some of the older tall roses (*Rosa centifolia* or *damascena* or *moschata*) for lasting fragrance. The multiflora rose, found in meadows and pastures but not truly wild, is the source of rose hips, which have many uses in decorations. Roses can be propagated from seeds, cuttings, or buddings, but it's easiest to buy nursery stock. Roses will grow well in a good, well-drained garden soil. Harvest rose hips in the fall when they turn red. Blossoms that you plan to dry should be picked on a day when the air is dry.

Preservation and Use

Hang roses and hips to dry for a short time; they really do not need glycerine treatment, although you may wish to spray them with plastic. They may be dried successfully by placing them in an arrangement or wreath without water. They will often dry with all their shape and color intact, but you must experiment with types. You can also hang them, place them on screens, or dry them in silica gel. Roses and rose hips have strong stems, but if you plan to wire them into wreaths, insert the wires while the roses are fresh because they may crumble when dry.

Rosemary
Rosmarinus officinalis

Young men and maids do ready stand
With sweet Rosemary in their hands
A perfect token of your Virgin's life.
—Roxburgh Ballads

Description

Rosemary is a tender perennial evergreen shrub with shining, needle-like leaves. It has a fragrance that we associate with Christmas, a spicy smell with a hint of ginger. This scent is released when the sun hits the leaves or when someone brushes the plant in passing.

Lore and Meaning

Constancy, fidelity, loyalty, enduring love, remembrance.

Culture and Harvest

Rosemary seed does not germinate well. It is easier started from cuttings or by layering. Plants grown in areas where winter temperatures drop below 10°F must be wintered inside in a cool window. Greenhouse plants need daily watering, but they should not be allowed to stand in water. You can harvest sprigs year round, but cut sparingly when growth is slow.

Preservation and Use

We use fresh rosemary in most Caprilands wreaths. Small bunches are inserted in herb and spice, wedding, and Victorian wreaths. It dries attractively in place and retains its color. Many people use rosemary from their wreaths for cooking, and so we avoid treating it with glycerine. For a finishing touch on a rosemary wreath, stick sprigs of rosemary into an apple and hang it from the bottom of the wreath. The moisture of the apple will help to preserve the herb branches.

Rowan
Sorbus aucuparia

The Hags returned,
To their Queen in sorrowful mood,
Crying that witches have no power
Where thrives the Rowan Tree wood.
—Old ballad

Description
The mountain ash, or rowan, is found from Newfoundland southward to North Carolina. It grows to about 30 feet at maturity. Its white spring flowers become very decorative clusters of red-orange berries in the fall.

Lore and Meaning
Protection, and good luck.

Culture and Harvest
Rowan trees can be propagated by seeds or by layering. They thrive in most soils. Harvest branches in the fall for berries.

Preservation and Use
Soak sprays of leaves and berries in a glycerine solution for two or three weeks; then spray the berries with lacquer so that they maintain their shape. Use the berries to decorate fall wreaths, and insert the sticks in witch's wreaths to ward off evil and protect the household.

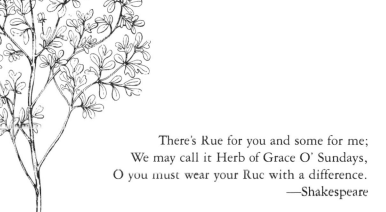

Rue
Ruta graveolens

There's Rue for you and some for me;
We may call it Herb of Grace O' Sundays,
O you must wear your Rue with a difference.
—Shakespeare

Description

Rue is a hardy perennial. Its aromatic foliage is bluish green, and the flowers are greenish yellow and resemble a cluster of stars. Its red-brown seedpods look hand carved. Glands found over the entire plant contain an oil that may cause skin irritation.

Lore and Meaning

Expels witches, infection, evil; mourning, sorrow, grace, virtue, and virginity.

Culture and Harvest

Rue is easily propagated form seed started indoors in the spring. It needs sunlight and a well-drained soil for best growth. Harvest leaves before the flowers form seed heads in fall.

Preservation and Use

Rue is the national plant of Lithuania. There, brides traditionally wear crowns of the fresh foliage over their veils. Bunches of rue also are pinned to their veils and to the coats of the grooms' attendants. The seed heads have decorative value, too. Their strong stems can be inserted into wreaths for an interesting touch.

Sage
Salvia officinalis

If the Sage tree thrives and grows
The master's not master and he knows.
—Anonymous

Description

Sage is a hardy perennial. Its firm oval leaves have a pebbly puckered surface. The stems and leaves have a pungent but pleasant fragrance and are covered with silver-gray hairs. In August purple flowers appear in whorls along the top of the stem.

Lore and Meaning

Youth, immortality, domestic virtue.

Culture and Harvest

Garden sage may be grown from seed, but make sure it is fresh; the seed stores poorly. Sage may also be propagated from division or cuttings. It thrives in moderately rich soil in full sun. Pick leaves when they are dry.

Preservation and Use

Sage leaves will curl as they dry, so you should press them between weighted papers. Experiment to see what works best for you. Handle the dried foliage carefully for it shatters easily. You can preserve sage in glycerine if you are sure that no one will remove it from the wreath to use in cooking. Once it has dried, you can tie bunches of it together and attach it to a wreath. At Caprilands, we add sage to many of the wedding wreaths.

Salad Burnet
Poterium sanguisorba

The even mead that erst brought sweetly forth
The freckled Cowslip, Burnet and green clover.
—Shakespeare

Description
Salad burnet is a hardy evergreen perennial that grows to one to three feet. The delicate, attractive leaves look somewhat like those of the wild rose, and remain nearly flat on the ground until flowering time. They smell like cucumber. The flowers are a deep, but pale, crimson and are clustered in rounded heads.

Lore and Meaning
Healing; encourages joy and gladness.

Culture and Harvest
Salad burnet grows easily from seed and thrives in full sun or partial shade in an average well-drained soil. Sow seeds in late fall or early spring. Use leaves fresh for the best cucumber aroma.

Preservation and Use
Burnet may be used fresh or dried. Hang stems to dry. Tied in little bunches and attached to wreaths, salad burnet gives off a nice scent. It can be woven into a braid of clover for necklaces for animals, as it was in midsummer festivals in northern Europe. We use burnet in our Caprilands kitchen wreath.

Thyme
Thymus vulgaris

Oh and I was a damsel so fair,
But fairer I wished to appear,
So I washed me in milk, and I dressed me in silk
And put the sweet thyme in my hair.
—Devonshire song

Description
Many varieties of thyme exist today. Some thymes are dark green; others are more gray or yellow. Some creep; others grow upward. Several have a distinctly citrus fragrance, but all have tiny oval leaves and many branches and grow close to the ground. *T. vulgaris* is the common thyme used to season foods and should be used in kitchen wreaths.

Lore and Meaning
Courage, elegance, energy.

Culture and Harvest
Thyme is a perennial and may be grown from seed in one season. Creeping thymes grow best from plant divisions. All need sun and good drainage. Harvest thyme when the dew has dried off.

Preservation and Use
The stems of thyme are too fine and short to force into wreaths, so you should wire cuttings together in small bunches. The lemon varieties are quite pliable and can easily be twined around a wire frame to form a wreath base. Thyme shrivels in drying, so be sure to use full bunches. Small kitchen wreaths made from bunches of thyme wired to a frame and tied with a bow make attractive gifts. Add measuring spoons or other small kitchen utensils to the bows as accents.

Vervain
Verbena officinalis

A wreath of Vervain heralds wear
Amongst our garlands named
Being sent that dreadful news to bear
Offensive war proclaimed.
—Drayton

Description
Vervain, with its blue flowery spikes, grows along highways in swampy areas. It is quite scarce today. The flower heads look like a pitch fork or trident. The leaves have an oblong to lancelike shape and are deeply divided.

Lore and Meaning
Enchantment; important to Romans and Druids. In German custom, a bride's hat is decorated with vervain, placing her under the protection of Venus.

Culture and Harvest
Vervain is hard to transplant, and it refuses to spread or winter over in the Caprilands gardens. Try to collect seed from the wild and plant it in a moist area. Vervain used to be so prized that there were specific rituals for harvesting. Look for its inconspicuous blossoms in July or August.

Preservation and Use
Vervain adds interest to wreaths with its meaning.

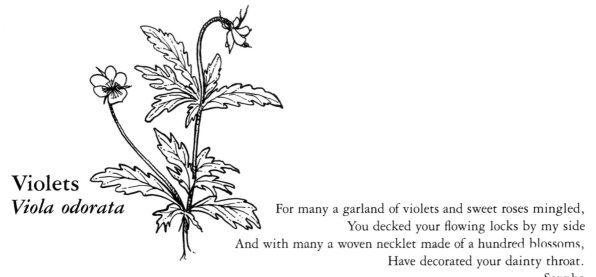

Violets
Viola odorata

For many a garland of violets and sweet roses mingled,
You decked your flowing locks by my side
And with many a woven necklet made of a hundred blossoms,
Have decorated your dainty throat.
—Sappho

Description
Violets have small but exquisite white to lavender, and even yellow, blossoms. The rich green leaves are heart shaped. This pervasive woodland plant signifies spring.

Lore and Meaning
Modesty, simplicity, honor.

Culture and Harvest
Violets are prolific and transplant well from woodlands or a friend's garden. They will self sow. Pick flowers for fresh use or for drying, or dig whole plants for living wreaths.

Preservation and Use
Violets can be dried in silica gel or borax, but they become very tiny and fragile. The best use of violets is in fresh small dainty wreaths. The stems are strong and pliable, sometimes quite long and are easily twined or braided into a circle.

Willow
Salix spp.

When once the lover's rose is dead
Or laid aside forlorne,
The willow garlands 'bout the head
Bedewed with tears are worn.
—Herrick

Description
Willows vary in size and have flexible branches that are used to make baskets or wreaths. The weeping willow (*Salix bubylonica*) is well known for its graceful pendulant branches. The leaves are long and slender. Willows seek water and grow best in moist environments.

Lore and Meaning
Sorrow.

Culture and Harvest
Cut the pliable branches whenever you need them. Pussy willow (*S. discolor*) branches may be harvested in spring when the catkins appear.

Preservation and Use
Willow branches are very pliable, and several can be combined and bound together with ribbon or willow strands. You can twist and bend the branches into a wreath or insert short pieces into a wreath base.

Yew
Taxus spp.

Old Yew! which graspeth at the stones
That name the underlying dead,
Thy fibres net the dreamless head,
Thy roots are wrapped about the bones.
—Tennyson

Description
The low-growing yews are among the most useful of the evergreens in making wreaths. The leaves are broader than those of fir or spruce and extend on either side of the stem to produce a flat effect. The rich, dark green foliage keeps its color throughout the year, and scarlet berries appear in fall.

Lore and Meaning
Everlasting life.

Culture and Harvest
Plant in spring before the new growth begins. Yews can be grown in a thin soil but do best in good, enriched earth. Harvest branches as you need them, and keep cuttings in water while you are working.

Preservation and Use
Of all evergreens used in holiday wreaths and garlands, yew lasts the longest. The needles do not fall off, and the branches remain oily and pliable.